CAMBRIDGE TEXTS AND STUDIES IN THE HISTORY OF EDUCATION

General Editors
A. C. F. BEALES, A. V. JUDGES, J. P. C. ROACH

T. H. HUXLEY ON EDUCATION

IN THIS SERIES

Texts

Studies

OTHER VOLUMES IN PREPARATION

ALSO BY CYRIL BIBBY

The Evolution of Man and his Culture
Heredity, Eugenics and Social Progress
Simple Experiments in Biology
Sex Education:
    A Guide for Parents, Teachers and Youth Leaders
How Life is Handed On
An Active Human Biology
Health Education:
    A Guide to Principles and Practice
A Healthy Day
Healthy and Happy
Healthy People
The Human Body
Race, Prejudice and Education
T. H. Huxley:
    Scientist, Humanist and Educator
The Essence of T. H. Huxley
The Biology of Mankind
Scientist Extraordinary:
    The Life and Scientific Work of T. H. Huxley

T. H. HUXLEY ON EDUCATION

A SELECTION FROM HIS WRITINGS
WITH AN INTRODUCTORY ESSAY AND NOTES BY

CYRIL BIBBY

Principal of Kingston upon Hull College of Education

CAMBRIDGE
AT THE UNIVERSITY PRESS
1971

Published by the Syndics of the Cambridge University Press
Bentley House, 200 Euston Road, London NW1 2DB
American Branch: 32 East 57th Street, New York, N.Y.10022

Library of Congress Catalogue Card Number: 72–154507

ISBN: 0 521 08061 4

Printed in Great Britain by
William Clowes & Sons Limited
London, Colchester and Beccles

FOR ALL TEACHERS WHO HATE
HUMBUG AND CANT AND ARE
THEREFORE ALSO EDUCATORS

CONTENTS

NOTE ON THE SELECTIONS

As always when making a limited selection from the writings of one who wrote much, it has been difficult to decide what to omit. One possibility would have been to print a few essays and lectures complete, thus gaining the benefit of a better presentation of some subjects at the cost of totally excluding others. Alternatively, one could print something from everything, thus providing wide coverage at the cost of crippling both literary effect and continuity of argument. Neither of these solutions seemed satisfactory. Instead, one item – 'A Liberal Education; and Where to Find it' – is presented in full while the others are abbreviated to varying degrees and in various manners.

From 'Emancipation – Black and White' a good deal has been omitted, including the preliminary references to Negro emancipation, but the gist of the argument for the reform of female education remains. 'The School Boards: What they Can do and What they May do' has been cut to about half its original length, the exclusions consisting largely of rebuttals of certain illiberal views which had been widely expressed during the election campaign. A considerable amount of 'Universities: Actual and Ideal' has had to be excised, but the essence of the argument remains. The 'Address on University Education' is pruned very heavily, but retains some interesting views on university teaching, examination and research, together with a brief but interesting consideration of medical education.

The shortening of those items which bear more especially on science education has been considered as a whole, so as to avoid mere duplication and yet give a picture of the manner in which their author tried to make the teaching of science into a complete cultural experience. These eight items ('On the Educational Value of the Natural

History Sciences', 'A Lobster; or, the Study of Zoology', 'On the Advisableness of Improving Natural Knowledge', 'Scientific Education: Notes of an After-dinner Speech', 'On the Study of Biology', 'On Elementary Instruction in Physiology', 'On Science and Art in Relation to Education', and 'Science and Culture') provide between them a striking presentation of what must surely be the core of the culture of tomorrow. Exigencies of space have, however, unfortunately necessitated the exclusion of much interesting material on the history and philosophy of science, to say nothing of some highly enjoyable polemic.

Two other items ('On the Hypothesis that Animals are Automata, and its History', and 'Hume') also hang together. In each case, the part presented is but a small fraction of the original whole – in the main, that part which bears on mental functioning, human behaviour and moral responsibility.

Finally, there are four items ('Administrative Nihilism', 'Technical Education', 'Address on Behalf of the National Association for the Promotion of Technical Education' and 'The Struggle for Existence in Human Society') which form some sort of a unity by reason of their bearings on general educational and social policy. They include discussions on natural and nurtural influences, on class prejudices, on educational delusions, on economic fallacies and on administrative realities, which seem as relevant today as when they were written.

The selections once made, it was almost equally difficult to decide in what order to present them. Huxley in his extremely busy life never produced a single comprehensive statement of his educational thinking, nor was that thinking conveniently compartmentalised to permit the easy grouping of individual addresses and essays. Whatever the ostensible subject, he almost always ranged into neighbouring fields, using whatever occasion presented itself as a peg on which to hang a complete garment from his harmonious educational wardrobe. Moreover – and this is evidence not of inflexibility of mind but of the early attainment of a synthetic outlook – his opinions on the fundamental pattern of a proper education changed but slightly during the thirty-five years spanned by these selections.

In the event, a simple chronological order has been adopted. This, of course, has certain obvious disadvantages; but it has the more than compensating advantage of allowing us to listen to a long symphony with recurrent variations on a few simple but potentially powerful themes.

C.B.

NOTE ON REFERENCES

Most of the quotations in the introductory essay are from three sources, which are abbreviated as follows:

C.E. *Collected Essays*, by T. H. Huxley (London: Macmillan, 1893–5)

H.P. Huxley Papers, in Archives of Imperial College of Science and Technology

L.L. *Life and Letters of Thomas Henry Huxley*, by L. Huxley (London: Macmillan, 1900)

In each case the abbreviation is followed by volume and page or folio numbers.

Other quotations come from official reports, which are abbreviated as follows:

C.C.   'Clarendon' Commission, *Report* (London, 1864)

G.C.   'Gresham' Commission, *Report* (London, 1894)

S.C.E.S.A. Select Committee on Education, Science and Art, *Report* (London, 1884)

S.C.P.S.B. Select Committee on the Public Schools Bill, *Report* (London, 1865)

S.C.S.I.   Select Committee on Scientific Instruction, *Report* (London, 1868)

U.L.C.D.S. University of London Committee on Degrees in Science, *Report* (London, 1858)

In each case the abbreviation is followed by answer or page number.

Yet others come from periodicals and newspapers, which are abbreviated as follows:

A.F.P.   *Aberdeen Free Press*

B.D.P.   *Birmingham Daily Post*

G.H.	*Glasgow Herald*
L.M.	*Liverpool Mercury*
M.G.	*Manchester Guardian*
N.	*Nature*
N.C.	*Nineteenth Century*
P.M.G.	*Pall Mall Gazette*
P.R.I.	*Proceedings of Royal Institution*
R.C.S.M.	*Royal College of Science Magazine*
S.B.C.	*School Board Chronicle*
S.L.P.	*South London Press*
T.	*The Times*
T.N.Y.A.S.	*Transactions of New York Academy of Sciences*
W.	*Witness*

In each case the abbreviation is followed by volume and/or issue and/or page numbers or by issue date.

Finally, a few quotations are from other books, which are abbreviated as follows:

Armstrong	*Our Need to Honour Huxley's Will*, by H. E. Armstrong (London: Macmillan, 1933)
Becker	*Scientific London*, by B. H. Becker (London: King, 1874)
Clodd	*Memories*, by E. Clodd (London, Chapman & Hall, 1916)
Farrar	*Men I Have Known*, by F. W. Farrar (New York: Crowell, 1897)
Huxley, L.	*Life and Letters of Sir Joseph Dolton Hooker*, by L. Huxley (London: Murray, 1918)
Huxley, T. H.	*Physiography; an Introduction to the Study of Nature*, by T. H. Huxley (London: Macmillan, 1877)
Manton	*Elizabeth Garrett Anderson*, by Jo Manton (London: Methuen, 1965)

Martin	*Life and Letters of the Rt. Hon. Robert Lowe, Viscount Sherbrooke*, by A. P. Martin (London: Longmans, 1893)
Montagu	*Man, his First Million Years*, by F. A. Montagu (New York: Signet Books, 1959)
Peterson	*Huxley: Prophet of Science*, by H. Peterson (New York: Longmans, 1932)
Smalley, *A.A.M.*	*Anglo-American Memories*, by G. W. Smalley, 2nd series (London: Duckworth, 1912)
Smalley, *L.L.*	*London Letters*, by G. W. Smalley (London: Macmillan, 1890)
Spencer	*Autobiography*, by H. Spencer (London: Williams & Norgate, 1904) (*sic*)
Wells	*Experiment in Autobiography*, by H. G. Wells (London: Gollancz & Cresset, 1934)

In each case the abbreviation is followed by volume and/or page number.

INTRODUCTORY ESSAY:
HUXLEY AS EDUCATOR

Thomas Henry Huxley was born on 4 May 1825, in rooms above a butcher's shop in what was then the pleasant little village of Ealing. George Huxley, his father, was a not very successful schoolmaster, from whom Thomas believed that he had inherited little but 'an inborn faculty for drawing . . . a hot temper, and that amount of tenacity of purpose which unfriendly observers sometimes called obstinacy' (*C.E.*, i, 4). His mother, Rachel, on the other hand, seems despite her lack of learning to have been a remarkable woman of excellent mental capacity. 'Her most distinguishing characteristic . . . was rapidity of thought. If one ventured to suggest she had not taken much time to arrive at a conclusion, she would say, "I cannot help it, things flash across me." That peculiarity has been passed on to me in full strength; it has often stood me in good stead; it has sometimes played me sad tricks, and it has always been a danger. But, after all, if my time were to come over again, there is nothing I should less willingly part with than my inheritance of mother-wit' (*ibid.*).

At the time of Huxley's birth, there was nothing that could be called a system of English education. Most children did not go to school at all. Of those who did, the majority picked up little more than elementary reading, writing and arithmetic at some deplorable dame establishment. The more fortunate might go to a school conducted by a local charity or by one of the two great voluntary societies, but in either case their education was likely to be less than mediocre. At a somewhat higher social level were the endowed schools, often enough poor shrunken relics of

[1]

better days and sometimes mere sinecures for their masters. Higher still were the exclusive 'public' schools, among which Eton was once described as a place where a boy might acquire a confirmed taste for gluttony and drunkenness, an aptitude for brutal sports and a passion for female society of the most degrading kind. As for the education of girls, it consisted mainly of acquirements either useful or amusing to men, and very few of the female sex were ever fortunate enough to receive any formal schooling. So far as higher education was concerned, Oxford was still under the statutes of 1638 and Cambridge under those of 1570, the former being characterised by Robert Lowe as 'governed academically and socially by what I can only describe as a clerical gerontocracy' (Martin, 1, 27).

Yet there were already a few faint first harbingers of change. While Huxley was a toddler of two, Brougham founded his Society for the Diffusion of Useful Knowledge, whose *Penny Magazine* was soon selling 200,000 copies per week. More and more self-educators and encyclopaedias came on the market, while the application of steam power to printing produced books cheaper and more numerous than ever before. Soon an intelligent and industrious child would be able to teach himself a great deal. In 1829 Thomas Arnold was appointed head of Rugby and began the cleaning up of the public schools. A year later University College (the 'godless college in Gower Street') was opened to break the established church's stranglehold on higher education. Three years after that, the further foundation of King's College in the Strand continued the process of providing London with credible alternatives to Oxbridge. In 1831 the British Association for the Advancement of Science was established, and soon the University of Durham began its five-year parturition. Finally, after readily voting £50,000 for improvements to the royal stables, Parliament somewhat reluctantly provided £20,000 as a grant in aid of schools. Things were as yet moving slowly; but indubitably they were moving.

At Ealing there was a private school, conducted by the formidable Dr Nicholas (the model for Thackeray's 'Dr Tickle-us'), with a social standing such that Prince Louis Philippe taught there during his exile from France. The mathematics master was George Huxley, and at the age of eight young Thomas (the seventh of eight children) was allowed to accompany his father and an elder brother to school. But he was miserably unhappy. 'Although my way of life has made me acquainted with all sorts and conditions of men from the highest to the lowest', he later wrote, 'I deliberately affirm that the society I fell into at school was the worst I have ever known ... the people who were set over us cared about as much for our intellectual and moral welfare as if they were baby-farmers. We were left to the operation of the struggle for existence among ourselves, and bullying was the least of the ill practices current among us' (*C.E.*, 1, 5). Perhaps he was unusually sensitive. Perhaps he suffered from the snubs and condescensions of socially superior school fellows – which may have contributed to his later declaration, 'I am a plebeian, and I stand by my order' (Smalley, *A.A.M.*, 19). Or he may have been especially baited as the son of a teacher, and of one so ineffective that apparently not a boy in the school knew the difference between an equilateral and an obtuse-angled triangle. At any rate, in 1835 his father gave up his job in somewhat obscure circumstances, and that was the end of young Tom Huxley's schooldays.

Leaving school after just two unhappy years, Huxley moved at the age of ten to Coventry, where his father supported the family by managing a small local savings bank. We know very little about what happened next. On one occasion Tom was discovered trying to read a German

book held in one hand while with the other he made hay
on a Warwickshire farm. At times he took part in discussions among adult friends and neighbours, on a variety of
intellectual topics. At the age of twelve he was wrapping
himself in a blanket and reading Hutton's *Geology* and
Hamilton's *Logic* with the aid of a candle when he was
supposed to be asleep. He tried to persuade his parents
that it was wrong to make dissenters pay church rates,
noting in a miniature home-made notebook that 'it is
against all laws of justice to force men to support a church
with whose opinions they cannot conscientiously agree.
The argument that the rate is so small is very fallacious. It
is as much a sacrifice of principle to do a little wrong as to
do a great one' (*L.L.*, 1, 10). He performed all manner of
elementary scientific experiment, including one 'to get
crystallised carbon. Got it deposited, but not crystallised'
(*ibid.*). He devoured Carlyle's *French Revolution* and
by him was led to German philosophy, this being 'one
half the debt he owed to Carlyle, the other half being
an intense hatred of shams of every sort and kind' (*ibid.*,
1, 9).

As a boy, Huxley wanted to be an engineer, but he never
got the chance. At the age of fifteen he was apprenticed to
a doctor in London's East End, where he 'used to wonder
sometimes why these people did not sally forth in mass and
get a few hours eating and drinking and plunder to their
hearts' content, before the police could stop and hang a
few of them' (*ibid.*, 1, 16). By this time the government had
opened its central School of Design, the University of
London had been established as an examining body,
James Kay (later Kay-Shuttleworth) had become the first
secretary of the Privy Council's Committee on Education,
and teacher-training colleges had been established in
Battersea and Chelsea. Then, in 1842, Huxley and one of
his brothers gained free scholarships for 'young Gentle-

men of respectable but unfortunate families' at Charing Cross Medical School.

Huxley's family was to prove more unfortunate than at that time could possibly have been foreseen. The admirable mother died of heart disease in 1852; the father was by then 'nearly lost to ... any other feeling beyond a vegetable existence' (H.P., 31.17); soon became 'sunk in worse than childish imbecility of mind' (*ibid.*, 31.21); and in 1855 died in an asylum. Sister Ellen's husband became 'a bloated mass of beer and opium' (*ibid.*, 31.24); brother George arrived at death's door as a result of 'extreme mental anxiety and incipient phthisis' (*ibid.*); brother William for some unexplained reason became totally estranged from the family; while brother James eventually became 'as near mad as a sane man can be' (*ibid.*, 31.44). Only Thomas and his favourite sister Lizzie seem to have led fairly normal lives – and even her husband was involved in some obscure muddle about a small legacy, changed his name, and emigrated with her to Tennessee. No wonder that Huxley's outlook on life was very different from that of most 'Eminent Victorians'!

But all this lay in the future, and meanwhile Huxley at the age of seventeen had a second chance of schooling. 'I am sorry to say', he later recalled, 'that I do not think any account of my doings as a student would tend to edification ... I worked extremely hard when it pleased me, and when it did not – which was a very frequent case – I was extremely idle (unless making caricatures of one's pastors and masters is to be called a branch of industry) or else wasted my energies in wrong directions' (*C.E.*, 1, 8). Still, he managed to walk off with several of the medical school's own prizes, to claim the Apothecaries' silver medal in open competition with the cream of University students, to take a gold in the First M.B. of London University, and to have his first research paper published by the age of twenty-one.

But by this time his free scholarship had come to an end, so he never graduated. (Apart, that is, from honorary degrees later conferred by Oxford, Cambridge, Edinburgh, Dublin, Breslau, Wurtzburg, Bologna and Erlangen.)

Faced in 1846 with the necessity of earning his daily bread, Huxley decided to join the Royal Navy, which in those days was not over-particular about the medical qualifications of those responsible for its sailors' health. Fortunately, his exceptional qualities were immediately recognised by the officer responsible for posting, who sent him not to a death-trap station in West Africa but to a donkey-frigate fitting out for exploration. Sailing in *Rattlesnake* as assistant-surgeon, which meant that he messed not with the officers but with the middies, Huxley somehow squeezed his five feet eleven into a cabin less than five feet high, with a small skylight into which his head projected. And that was his home for the next four years. Cockroach-ridden and leaking at the seams, his ship sailed south to the Cape, west to Rio, down to Australia, and then cruised along the Great Barrier Reef towards New Guinea. In these conditions, with not much more than a wire-mesh meat-cover for trawl and with his microscope securely lashed to the chart-room table, Huxley examined the delicate translucent organisms of the southern seas. With no teacher and very few books of reference, he packeted back home from successive ports a series of research papers of peculiar brilliance. At the age of twenty-five, within a few months of *Rattlesnake*'s return to England, he was elected Fellow of the Royal Society. It no longer seemed so important that he was a non-graduate.

These years afloat were not without significance for Huxley's views on education. At a time when most students relied almost entirely upon professorial or printed authority, he found out facts for himself and became profoundly suspicious of all merely traditional teaching. He learned that life was well worth living even when 'one woke up from a night's rest on a soft plank, with the sky for canopy and cocoa and weavilly biscuit the sole prospect for breakfast' (*C.E.*, I. 13), and that it was worthwhile 'to work for the sake of what I got for myself out of it, even if it all went to the bottom and I along with it' (*ibid.*). And he formed the firm conviction that 'the ascertainable is infinitely greater than the ascertained . . . the chief business of the teacher is not so much to make scholars as to train pioneers' (*N.*, 2897, 707). Naturally, he was often irked by the attitudes and intellectual limitations of naval officers brought up from the age of thirteen to worship the Queen's regulations and instructions; but he also found that, 'whether . . . book-learned or not, they were emphatically men, trained to face realities and to have a wholesome contempt for mere talkers. Any one of them was worth a wilderness of phrase-crammed undergraduates' (*L.L.*, II, 264). And, although he sometimes resented the severity of naval discipline on shipboard, he nevertheless came to believe that 'Perhaps the most valuable result of all education is the ability to make yourself do the thing you have to do, when it ought to be done, whether you like it or not' (*C.E.*, III, 414).

While Huxley was occupied first as medical student and then as assistant-surgeon, the organisation of English education proceeded apace. Before *Rattlesnake* set sail, there were already a couple of hundred Mechanics' Institutes scattered across the face of the land, the number of training colleges had increased to over twenty, and the pupil-teacher system was well established. Middle-class schools had been founded in Birmingham, Hull, Leicester and other provincial cities, soon to be followed by proprietory boarding schools such as Cheltenham and Marlborough. In 1848, F. D. Maurice and his friends established Queen's College in Harley Street for the education of females, to be joined a year later by Bedford Square College. From the former emerged Miss Buss and Miss Beale, the one to build up the North London Collegiate School for Girls and the other to become headmistress of Cheltenham Ladies College. In 1850, the year of *Rattlesnake*'s return, the government's School of Mines opened its doors in Jermyn Street and a Royal Commission was constituted to inquire into the affairs of Oxford and Cambridge.

Before he had been long back home, Huxley was everywhere acknowledged as the young eagle of British biology. Powerful people pulled strings to secure him paid leave from naval duties so that he could concentrate on research, which he did to immense effect for the next three years. But back in Australia there was Henrietta Anne Heathorn, with whom he had fallen instantly in love at a dance ashore, and they were both waiting impatiently for the time when they could afford to marry. Towards the end of 1851, Huxley wrote to a friend in Sydney, 'here in England the fighting and scratching to keep your place in the crowd exclude almost all other thoughts' (H.P., 30.31). However, he added, 'When I last wrote I was but at the edge of the crush at the pit door of this great fools theatre – now I have worked my way into it, and through it, and am I hope not far from the check takers' (*ibid.*). Nevertheless, he failed to get chairs at Toronto, Aberdeen, Cork and King's College, London, and even contemplated emigrating to Australia where there was a job with a brewer. Then, in 1854, and just as he faced financial catastrophe by being struck off the Navy List for refusing to accept a posting which would have interfered with his research, he secured a part-time lectureship in palaeontology at the School of Mines. Other part-time sources of income were soon added, and Nettie set sail for England. They married in 1855 and lived happily ever after.

It quickly became clear that Huxley was a teacher to his fingertips. 'As a class lecturer', wrote one student, 'Huxley was *facile princeps* ... Clear, deliberate, never hesitant or unduly emphatic, never repetitional, always logical, his every word told' (*R.C.S.M.*, VIII, 3). Another recalled 'that rich fund of humour ever ready to swell forth when occasion permitted, sometimes accompanied with an extra gleam in his bright dark eyes, sometimes expressed with a dryness and gravity of look which gave it a double zest' (*N.C.*, XLII, 990). Yet another remembered how students 'sat in the face of his blackboard and watched him embroider it most exquisitely with chalks of varied hue; the while he talked like a book; with absolute precision, in chosen words' (Armstrong, 6).

Yet Huxley knew that the true educator must be much more than a good lecturer. 'Teaching in England', he told the 1868 Select Committee on Scientific Instruction, 'is pretty much a matter of chance, and the mass of the people are ignorant of the fact that there is such a thing as a scientific method of teaching' (S.C.S.I., 8000). And, he said, 'An important defect in the School of Mines is that in the great majority of cases, the entire business of teaching is thrown upon the professors ... that is to say, we have not the tutorial system as well as the professorial system, though both of these systems ought to be combined in any completely organised course of instruction' (*ibid.*, 7959). So he conducted his own classes as a careful combination of lecturing, demonstrating, questioning, stimulating, examining, and on occasion rebuking. And eventually, when new laboratories provided the necessary facilities, he established England's first thoroughly pedagogic system of individual practical instruction in science.

Even as an adolescent, Huxley had noted for his own guidance, 'let me remember this – that it is better to read a little and thoroughly than cram a crude undigested mass into my head, though it be great in quantity' (*L.L.*, I, 11). Thirty-odd years later, in some unpublished lecture notes, he made much the same point, but added the desirability of balance between teacher-selected and pupil-selected content: 'There is far too much of the feeding-bottle in education & young people ought to be supplied with good intellectual food and then left to help themselves' (H.P., 39.89). His ideal was that favourite saying cut in stone on the memorial plaque at Ealing, 'Try to learn something about everything and everything about something.'

A German investigator of English education once remarked, 'Professor Huxley loves to make his students begin at the beginning. A thorough believer in human ignorance and stupidity, he takes utter and complete ignorance for granted' (Becker, 181). He could, moreover, be pretty cutting, as when one student's unworthy laboratory diagram was briefly assessed with the comment, 'I am glad to know it is a liver; it reminds me as much of Cologne cathedral in a fog as of anything' (*T.N.Y.A.S.*, xv, 40). Yet innumerable reminiscences praise his helpfulness to all who genuinely wished to learn, and his ruthlessness to error seems rarely to have aroused resentment. One of his last students, H. G. Wells (in whose *Anne Veronica* he is readily recognisable as 'Professor Russell') affirmed, 'That year I spent in Huxley's class was, beyond all question, the most educational year in my life. It left me under that urgency for coherence and consistency, that repugnance for hap-hazard assumptions and arbitrary statements, which is the essential distinction of the educated from the uneducated mind' (Wells, 199).

Although tempted by many an offer elsewhere, Huxley was to spend the rest of his working life at the institution to which he first went as a part-time teacher at £100 per annum. Quickly becoming indispensable and by reason of sheer ability exercising continually increasing power, he soon felt able to tell a friend, 'To speak nautically, I have been there long enough to "know the ropes" – and I shall take pleasure in working the place into what I think it ought to be' (H.P., 15.102). So, instead of moving to posts of higher repute, he simply stayed where he was and made the school into something worthy of him. Attracting both students and colleagues of the highest ability, and operating with immense skill along the complex corridors of power, he more than any man converted the little School of Mines into the fine new Normal School of Science at South Kensington, where it grew first into the great Royal College of Science and eventually into the mighty Imperial College of Science and Technology.

From this scientific sacrarium he sent out through the years a steady stream of young disciples who carried his message across half the world. And, of course, there were the hundreds of thousands who read his textbooks. As a young man, he had started writing because he badly needed the money to maintain his wife and family, and no doubt financial considerations continued to count. But, increasingly, his motivation became that of providing simple yet thoroughly scientific replacements for what he once described as 'detestable books which ought to have been burned by the hands of the common hangman' (*C.E.*, III, 170). In 1864 there appeared *Elements of Comparative Anatomy* and the *Elementary Atlas of Comparative Osteology*, both for specialist students but each of crystalline clarity. Two years later came *Lessons in Elementary Physiology*, eulogised by Kay-Shuttleworth for its simplicity and superbly demonstrating that Huxley's was a pen for popularisation. During the next decade there were the *Introduction to the Classification of Animals*, the *Anatomy of Vertebrated Animals*, the *Course of Practical Instruction in Elementary Biology* and the *Anatomy of Invertebrated Animals*. Then, in 1877, that little gem of a school text,

Physiography, which sold 3,000 copies in its first six weeks and went through seventeen printings in as many years. With editions appearing through the years in French, German, Hungarian, Polish, Portuguese and Russian, Huxley's textbooks exerted a world-wide educational influence which it is almost impossible to over-estimate.

Alongside his always conscientious teaching and his prolific writing, Huxley maintained a massive programme of research. He always held that 'the future of the world lies in the hands of those who are able to carry the interpretation of nature a step further than their predecessors ... the highest function of a university is to seek out those men, cherish them, and give their ability to serve their kind full play' (*ibid.*, III, 254). But he never confused the highest function with the major function, and he would have given short shrift to any of his staff who neglected their students on account of their researches. Moreover, he believed that 'the best investigators are usually those who have also the responsibilities of instruction' (*ibid.*, III, 255), and that the need to bring things to a point for the benefit of students was a powerful prophylactic against both arrogance and sloth.

During Huxley's first ten years at the School of Mines, England's educational system was making major advances. Shortly before he started at Jermyn Street, the Natural Sciences Tripos had been established at Cambridge, Owens College had been founded in Manchester, the Department of Science and Art had been set up under the Board of Trade, and the Working Men's College had opened in north London. Soon the Oxford and Cambridge University Acts were to force reform on the ancient universities, Newman to inaugurate his roman catholic university in Dublin, and Edinburgh to be granted its Regius Chair of Technology. In 1855 the Society of Arts created its country-wide system of examinations, while in the following year the government grant for schools amounted to nearly half a million pounds. Also in 1856, the Privy Council took over the Department of Science and Art from the Board of Trade and thus began to provide something at least approaching an embryonic Ministry of Education. A couple of years later, the first Oxford and Cambridge Local Examinations were held; in 1859 the Newcastle Commission on Elementary Education was appointed, soon to be followed by the Clarendon Commission on the Public Schools. Then, in 1864, both the Taunton Commission on Endowed Schools and the Argyll Commission on Scottish Schools began their work; while Robert Lowe, whose 'Revised Code' and 'Payment by Results' had so sterilised the development of imaginative education, resigned his position as Vice-President of the Committee of Council.

During this same period, Huxley's own development had also proceeded apace. By 1864 he was a solid family man, living with his wife and five children (Jessie, Marian, Leonard, Rachel and Nettie) in a substantial house in Marylebone. His income had reached £950 plus royalties – and a pound in those days was still a valuable golden sovereign. He had served as Lecturer in Anatomy at St Thomas's Hospital, Fullerian Professor at the Royal Institution, Examiner to the University of London, Croonian Lecturer, Secretary of the Geological Society and Hunterian Professor at the Royal College of Surgeons– all, of course, on top of his permanent post at the School of Mines. And, despite his uncompromising refusal to submit to any type of entrenched authority, his scientific eminence and personal charm were such that he had been elected in 1858 to the Athenaeum at the head of the poll under the 'distinguished persons' rule.

Huxley seems never quite to have got over his surprise at the way in which he was so soon accepted in the most distinguished circles despite his outspoken expression of unorthodox views. 'I will leave my mark somewhere', he had told his sister Lizzie almost immediately upon his return to England in *Rattlesnake*, 'and it shall be clear and distinct T. H. H., HIS MARK and free from the abominable blur of cant, humbug and self-seeking which surrounds this present world' (*L.L.*, 1, 60). It is difficult to be certain how successfully he avoided all self-seeking as the years went by, but there are not many who have managed so well as he did to keep clear of cant and humbug throughout an adult lifetime of scarcely diluted success. Everyone has heard of his historic 1860 clash with the Bishop of Oxford over Darwin's theory, but this was only the most famous of innumerable occasions when he refused to compromise with religious, scientific, social or educational obscurantism. 'Fancy unco' guid Edinburgh requiring illumination on the subject!', he wrote to his wife when invited to speak at that city's Philosophical Institute. 'They know my views, so if they do not like what I shall have to tell them, it is their own fault' (*ibid.*, 1, 192). And he was probably not very surprised when the presbyterian *Witness* described his lecture as being 'in blasphemous contradiction to biblical narrative and doctrine . . . the vilest and beastliest paradox ever vented in ancient or modern times among Pagans or Christians' (*W.*, 11.1.62).

But Huxley was as outspoken against orthodoxy in other fields as in religion, and seems scarcely ever to have refrained from saying exactly what he thought. In 1867, addressing the Mayor and assembled civic worthies of Birmingham, he reminded them that the early Britons must have seemed as uncivilised to the invading Romans as more recently the Maoris had to the English; said that he himself had met in Australia a very intelligent black-fellow, 'who was certainly, he believed, as good a man as one-half of the British Philistines' (*B.D.P.*, 12.10.67); and asserted that there was no biological evidence that racial interbreeding was necessarily harmful. In 1871 he publicly informed a comfortable spa community that he 'did not care to address a dilettante audience such as Leamington was likely to afford' (H.P., 30.172), yet he gladly travelled up to give a lecture in Liverpool to aid the funds of a working-class trades council. It is perhaps not surprising that, despite his own not very revolutionary political views, there were sometimes complaints that he gave encouragement to 'socialist agitators'. Much later, when Oxford appointed the philologist Napier to its newly instituted English chair, Huxley publicly denounced the move and declared that 'the establishment of professorial chairs of philology, under the name of literature, may be a profit to science, but is really a fraud practised upon letters' (P.M.G., 20.10.86). Later still, when the great new federal University of London was being planned, he warned against the creation of 'an Established Church Scientific, with a hierarchical organisation and a Professorial Episcopate' (L.L., II, 315). Towards the very end of his life, he recalled the storms of earlier days and their eventual unexpected outcome: 'The Boreas of criticism blew his hardest blasts of misrepresentation and ridicule for some years, and I was as one of the wicked. Indeed, it surprises me at times to think how anyone who had sunk so low could since have emerged into at any rate relative respectability' (C.E., VII, x).

In his very brief autobiographical essay, Huxley explained, 'I [was not] endowed with that mellifluous eloquence which, in this country, leads far more surely than worth, capacity, or honest work, to the highest places in Church and State . . . and I have been obliged to content myself through life with saying what I mean in the plainest of plain language, than which, I suppose, there is no habit more ruinous to a man's prospects of advancement' (ibid., I, 3). But his wry smile shines right through this statement: the truth is that he positively revelled in plain speaking, especially to the pompous. As he once confessed to Lizzie, 'I have a high standard of excellence, and am no respecter of persons, and I am afraid I show the latter peculiarity rather too much' (*L.L.*, I, 158). This propensity alone could have done little more than make enemies; but it was not alone. It was accompanied by a passionate belief that the proclamation of truth was not merely a social desideratum but the first of the moral virtues, by a remarkable mastery of facts and clarity of vision, by an early life remote from the established schools and universities which so blinkered most educators of his generation, and by an empathy with the workers which enabled him to avoid all condescension in his proposals for their education. And, of course, by that personal charm which permitted him to express devastating truths without giving personal offence. 'I like to speak to Mr. Huxley', said the most accomplished of Queen Victoria's daughters, 'because he talks to me exactly as he would to any other woman' (Smalley, *LL.*, II, 110).

One of the first things Huxley did after going to the School of Mines was to reorganise its Museum of Practical Geology, and this was the beginning of his belief that properly planned and conducted museums could play an important part in popular education. 'I think it would be desirable', he submitted to the Director in 1855, 'to form two catalogues the one of which might be termed the Popular Catalogue & the other the Official Catalogue. The former of these would be intended to serve as an explanation of the nature & meaning of the collections to the general Public who visit it – To this end I should propose to write an elementary & popular account of the most characteristic animals of each great formation – illustrated by woodcuts' (H.P., 23.143). Three years later he wrote to his friend Hooker, 'It is true that the people stroll through the enormous collections of the British Museum, but the sole result is that they are dazzled and confused by the multiplicity of unexplained objects' (*L.L.*, 1, 134), and he wanted distinct provision made for the research scientist and the man in the street. In 1859 he gave advice to Warwick on the organisation of its museum, as he later did in various other places including Cambridge. He advised Manchester that the public collection should be 'large enough to illustrate all the most important truths of Natural History, but not so extensive as to weary or confuse ordinary visitors' (*L.L.*, 1, 135). And to Chester he wrote deploring 'the ordinary lumber-room of clubs from New Zealand, sharks' teeth, mangy monkeys, scorpions and conch-shells – who shall describe the weary inutility of it ?' (*ibid.*, 1, 136). Trudging today through many a museum, who would imagine that all this sound sense had already been written so long ago ?

In 1874 Huxley was involved in a move to bring the national museums and art galleries under parliamentary control, to extend their benefits to local museums throughout the country, and to make them bear on public education. This proposal was only partially implemented, but it was decided to transfer the scientific sections of the British Museum to a new building, in whose planning Huxley played a prime part and which established the first national loan-collection of scientific apparatus and teaching materials. Speaking at its opening, he gently mocked the usual sort of museum, where 'You have walked through a quarter of a mile of animals, more or less well stuffed, with their long names written out underneath them; and unless your experience is very different from that of most people, the upshot of it all is that you leave that splendid pile with sore feet, a bad headache, and a general idea that the animal kingdom is a "mighty maze without a plan"' (*C.E.*, III, 287). Presumably he had already told Robert Lowe what he believed a museum should be, for after dinner one day in the spring of 1863 he amusedly noted, 'our friend Bob is a most admirable, well-judging statesman, for he says I am the only man fit to be at the head of the British Museum, and that if he had his way he would put me there' (*L.L.*, I, 248).

Huxley never had any doubt about the wide variance of innate abilities, and as an administrator he believed that 'it is mere ruin to any service to let [seniority] interfere with the promotion of men of marked superiority' (*ibid.*, II, 295). But he also believed that 'The attainment of both health and wisdom may be promoted or hindered to an almost indefinite extent by education' (H.P., 42.76), and this belief strengthened his resolve to open up new educational opportunities for the underprivileged. And, to those who seemed so confident that it was possible to prejudge the eventual development of children, he said, 'I doubt whether even the keenest judge of character, if he had before him a hundred boys and girls under fourteen, could pick out, with the least chance of success, those who should be kept, as certain to be serviceable members of the polity, and those who should be chloroformed, as equally sure to be stupid, idle, or vicious. The "points" of a good or of a bad citizen are really far harder to discern than those of a puppy or a short-horn calf' (*C.E.*, IX, 23). Moreover, although nobody ever had a higher regard for intelligence than him, he told the medical students of University College that 'patience and tenacity of purpose are worth more than twice their weight of cleverness' (*ibid.*, III, 306).

In his contributions to working-class education, therefore, Huxley took immense trouble to express complex ideas simply, but never indulged in the sort of 'popularisation' which implicitly assumed inferiority in his audience – the type of thing which he derided as 'a sort of dinner given from the soup-kitchen of science to the intellectually poor' (*G.H.*, 17.2.76). He once wrote to a friend, 'I believe in the fustian, and can talk to it better than to any amount of gauze and Saxony' (H.P., 15.62). It was this genuine concern for the education of the ordinary people which led Huxley to serve as honorary (but far from inactive) Principal of the South London Working Men's College from its foundation in 1868 until 1880. And it is surely fitting that, among the eventual progeny of this place at which he delivered his classic opening address, 'A Liberal Education; and Where to Find it', there were not only a technical college and a school of art and crafts, but also a day school for older girls and women, the first free library south of the river, and an art gallery.

It was not vanity, but simple regard for fact, which led Huxley to tell a Liverpool audience, 'I can certainly claim for myself that sort of mental temperament which can say that nothing human comes amiss to it. I have never yet met with any branch of human knowledge which I have found unattractive ... and I have yet to meet with any form of art in which it has not been possible for me to take as acute a pleasure as, I believe, it is possible for men to take' (*C.C.*, III, 164). This, no doubt, is why Lord Avebury among others believed that 'Huxley was one of those all-round men who would have succeeded in any walk of life' (*N.*, LXIII, 92). Moreover, Huxley believed that most people had the potential for a wide range of studies, and he told the Select Committee on Education, Science and Art that 'a man of average faculties may be trained in one direction to literature or in another to science; and he ought to be able to devote himself to either if he is properly taught' (S.C.E.S.A., 1716). Further, he said, 'I do not disguise my conviction that the whole theory on which our present educational system is based, is wrong from top to bottom; that the subjects which are now put down as essential ... are luxuries, so to speak; and that those which are regarded as comparatively un-essential and as luxuries are the essentials' (*ibid.*, 1708).

For Huxley, the chief essentials of education were litera-ture, history, political economy and science; and he could conceive no truly liberal education in which they did not all play important parts. As early as 1858 he had told the University of London that 'the time is rapidly approaching when no person who is not moderately conversant with scientific matters will be able to take part in ordinary conversation, or to consider himself an educated person' (U.L.C.D.S., 66). But, he immediately added, 'the great danger which Science has to avoid is the one-sidedness of those who follow it' (*ibid.*). In 1870, as still to some extent a century later, there was a widespread tendency for arts graduates to give themselves airs as being 'liberally' educated, and it was salutary for a Senate committee to be told, 'I venture to think that it would be as great a scandal that any person possessing a University degree in Arts should be ignorant of the law of gravitation ... as that a B.Sc. should be ignorant of Cromwell's existence' (H.P., 42.34). Huxley would have agreed with Moberley's com-ment to the Clarendon Commission, that a scientific fact is 'simply a barren fact ... it does not germinate, it is a perfectly unfruitful fact' (C.C., 494); but he would have said precisely the same of a simple fact in any other field of study. And he rejected as inadequate Matthew Arnold's thesis, that the meaning of culture was to know the best that has been thought and said in the world, for it left out of account all culture which cannot be expressed in words.

In his *Man's Place in Nature*, Huxley had written, 'The question of questions for mankind – the problem which underlies all others, and is more deeply interesting than any other – is the ascertainment of the place which Man occupies in nature and of his relations to the universe of things. Whence our race has come; what are the limits of our power over nature, and of nature's power over us; to what goal we are tending; are the problems which present themselves anew and with undiminished interest to every man born into the world' (*C.E.*, VII, 77). Moreover, he maintained at the opening of Birmingham's Mason College in 1880, 'this scientific "criticism of life" presents itself to us with different credentials from any other. It appeals not to authority, nor to what anybody may have thought or said, but to nature. It admits that all our interpretations of natural fact are more or less imperfect, and symbolic, and bids the learner seek for truth not among words but among things' (*ibid.*, III, 150). So, when he came to consider what constituted a liberal education, he was as willing to find it in a well-conducted vocational or professional course as in one more abstracted from the realities of daily existence. That was why, when speaking in Baltimore at the opening of Johns Hopkins University in 1876, he declared that 'any man who has seriously studied all the essential branches of medical knowledge; who has the needful acquaintance with the elements of physical science; who has been brought by medical jurisprudence into contact with law; whose study of insanity has taken him into the fields of psychology; has *ipso facto* received a liberal education' (*ibid.*, III, 249). Nor had he any time at all for that tendency, still endemic in academic circles, to elevate in estimation whatever may be useless. Indeed, he declared, 'there is no position so ignoble as that of the so-called "liberally educated practitioner", who may be able to read Galen in the original; who knows all the plants, from the cedar of Lebanon to the hyssopp upon the wall; but who finds himself, with the issues of life and death in his hands, ignorant, blundering, and bewildered' (*ibid.*). It was with views like these that in 1870 Huxley set about securing for the street arabs of England's sprawling metropolis an education that was at the same time liberal and of practical use.

The second lustrum of the 1860s had seen many significant educational advances. At Exeter and elsewhere the seeds of future university colleges were sown in the form of small local institutions of higher education. In Isleworth the International College (with Huxley as one of its governors) began in 1866 a fascinating educational experiment in advance of anything we have today. There was Dean Farrar's 1867 *Essays on a Liberal Education*, there were Matthew Arnold's *Schools and Universities on the Continent* and his *Culture and Anarchy*, there was Mark Pattison's *Suggestions on Academical Organisation*. In 1868 the Public Schools Act was passed, the Select Committee on Scientific Instruction began its investigations, and degrees in science and technology were instituted at Edinburgh. The following year saw the first of the Endowed Schools Acts, the opening of Girton College for the university education of women, and the establishment both of the Headmasters' Conference and of the secular National Education League. But the greatest need of all, a system of schooling for the children of the ordinary people, had always been held up by the conflicting interests of the competing religious sects. Then, in 1870, W. E. Forster's great new Education Act provided for the election of local School Boards, and Huxley stood as a candidate in Marylebone.

Without any established organisation to back him or sufficient funds for any substantial campaign, anathema to many on account of his agnosticism, Huxley might have seemed to destroy whatever slim chances he had by running in harness with a radical carpenter who had been one of Garibaldi's reception committee. Nor did he mince words when telling one of his few meetings that 'no breeder would bring up his pigs under such conditions as those to which the poorer classes of England were now subjected' (*T.*, 22.11.70). Still less, one might have thought, could it have helped, that his election address, directed to exclusively householder voters, declared, 'It seems to be the fashion for Candidates to assure you that they will do their best to spare the poverty of the Ratepayers. It is proper, therefore, for me to add that I can give you no such assurance on my own behalf . . . my vote will be given for that expenditure which can be shown to be just and necessary, without any reference to the question whether it may raise the rate a halfpenny' (H.P.).

It says much for the ratepayers of Marylebone that they elected Huxley. It says even more for the overwhelmingly church-going members of the Board that, almost immediately, they made him chairman of their all-important Scheme of Education Committee. From this emerged that pattern of infant, junior and senior schools which spread right across the land and lasted until the Act of 1944. It established that the curriculum of Board schools should be much wider than many had expected, that there should be defined standards of hygiene, that corporal punishment should be discouraged and strictly controlled, and that the professional authority of the teacher should be protected from excessive interference by Board members. And all this was accomplished within a mere fourteen months, during which Huxley attended some 170 meetings of miscellaneous committees, travelled about the country in search of isolated examples of good schooling worthy of emulation, pulled every powerful string he could lay hands on – and eventually suffered total collapse requiring lengthy convalescence in Italy and Egypt. Much later he was to declare, 'I am glad to think that, after all these years, I can look back upon that period of my life as perhaps the part of it least wasted' (*C.E.*, III, 431).

In his December 1870 *Contemporary Review* article, 'The School Boards: What they Can do, and What they May do', Huxley had outlined his scheme of education. First he asked for physical training, and he advised the Board that 'as broad an interpretation as possible should be given to the term [drill]' (*S.B.C.*, II, 167). Next came domestic economy, especially but not exclusively for girls. Then there was the preparation of pupils for their eventual rôle as responsible citizens by means of education in social science, which he had earlier described as 'what may be called the natural laws of conduct, or the laws which govern the organization of society ... the conditions of social organization; the natural basis of morality' (S.C.S.I., 7988). Reading, writing and arithmetic, to which some would have confined the instruction of the poor, were to be accompanied by wider studies; for, as Huxley said at an early Board meeting, 'the Revised Code, which produces instruction in the tools of learning and denies any fragment of real knowledge when you have got the tools ... is a sort of system which might be described as the teaching a carpenter to go through the motions of the saw and plane, yet never let him have wood to work upon' (*S.B.C.*, I, 8). Naturally there was to be instruction in elementary science, of which the pupils should be quite capable since 'children of high natural ability ... are just as abundant among the poor as among the rich' (*C.E.*, III, 400). There was to be drawing, and there was to be music, which latter he described as 'one of the most civilising and enlightening influences which a child can be brought under' (*S.B.C.*, I, 8).

Most people were very surprised when Huxley supported classroom reading of the Bible. In 1863 he had told Charles Kingsley, 'I go into society, and except among two or three of my scientific colleagues I find myself alone on these subjects, and as hopelessly at variance with the majority of my fellow-men as they would be with their neighbours if they were set down among the Ashantees. I don't like this state of things for myself – least of all do I see how it will work out for my children' (*L.L.*, I, 239). By 1870, however, his first five offspring had been followed by Henry and Ethel, Jessie was already entering her teens, and Huxley had learned a lot about children and their upbringing. Moreover, although he never had any real doubt that 'the principle of strict secularity in State education is sound, and must ultimately prevail' (*ibid.*, I, 343), he recognised also that the 1870 Act was a compromise and he 'desired simply to administer this Act as an honest man, according to the letter and spirit of the law, and not to throw difficulties into the way of its operation' (*T.*, 22.11.70). And, although he told the Board that, 'If . . . they had to deal with a fresh and untouched population . . . it would not enter into his mind to introduce the religious and ethical ideal by the agency of . . . the Bible' (*S.B.C.*, I, 44), he also believed that a people's moral education must be by 'a system connected with or not too widely divorced from their own system and beliefs' (*ibid.*). After all, as he had remarked in his *Contemporary* article, 'Nine-tenths of a dose of bark is mere half-rotten wood; but one swallows it for the sake of the particles of quinine' (*C.E.*, III, 396). Furthermore, he told a friend a few years later, 'my meaning was that the mass of the people should not be deprived of the one great literature which is open to them – nor shut out from the perception of their relation with the whole past history of civilised mankind' (Clodd, 41). Finally, as he retrospectively explained to Lord Farrer in 1894, 'Twenty years of reasonably good primary education is "worth a mass"' (*L.L.*, II, 283).

Apart from his election to the first London School Board, Huxley had in 1870 been elected President of the British Association, appointed to the Devonshire Commission on Scientific Instruction, nominated by the Committee of Privy Council as a governor of Owens College, and been honoured by the Moscow Imperial Natural History Society. In 1871, the year in which certain religious tests were abolished at Oxford and Cambridge, he got his new laboratories at South Kensington, became Secretary of the Royal Society, turned down an invitation to stand for Parliament, conducted England's first course in practical biology for schoolteachers, and tried to persuade Gladstone to use the magnificent buildings of Greenwich Hospital for a technical university. It was in this year that Hooker wrote despairingly to Darwin, 'his love of exercising his marvellous intellectual power over men is leading him on – and on – and on – God knows to where – here he is now, at Owens' College, Manchester, on Friday, and lecturing again to working men at Liverpool yesterday, and to be back in London tonight!' (L. Huxley, II, 125). Eventually the strain began to tell, but nothing could stop Huxley from working full-out between his periodic bouts of medically enforced rest.

After recovering from the breakdown brought about by his heroic endeavours on the London School Board, Huxley returned to England early in the summer of 1872. He was doubtless delighted that Joseph Payne, whose earlier lectures at the College of Preceptors he had supported, had become England's first Professor of Education. He was almost immediately involved in selecting a science Fellow for Exeter College, Oxford, to which he sent that stormy petrel Ray Lankester. But his most important new undertaking that year was the Rectorship of Aberdeen University. A group of students invited him to stand on a platform of university reform and, against *ad hominem* attacks of impressive scurrility, by almost every obscurantist in his opponent's territorial city, he defeated the 'Cock o' the North', the young Marquess of

Huntley. He succeeded beyond expectation in mustering support for his proposed reforms, and after one Court meeting wrote to his wife in great glee: 'Did I tell you that I carried all my resolutions about improving the medical curriculum ? Fact, though greatly to my astonishment. To-morrow we go in for some reforms in the arts curriculum, and I expect that the job will be tougher' (*L.L.*, 1, 408). But the academic traditionalists displayed all their ancient skills in the tactics of delay, which even included an opposing petition to the Privy Council from the University of Edinburgh. In 1876 a Royal Commission on the Universities of Scotland was set up – and probably nobody was particularly surprised to see Huxley turning up as one of its members. It reported very much along his lines, thus justifying the prophecy which he had made in his 1874 rectorial address, that his defeats would become victories in the hands of his successors.

Meanwhile, the Girls' Public Day School Company had been formed, Cambridge University had started its Extension lectures, the Yorkshire College had been founded in Leeds, and Huxley had received honorific fellowships from scientific and cultural societies in Germany, Italy, New Zealand, Sweden, Belgium, Portugal and the U.S.A. As a governor of the reconstituted Owens College, he had worked closely with Kay-Shuttleworth (and on some issues with Matthew Arnold) to see that from the start the right people were appointed to the College Council. He had brought forward the question of the more methodical teaching of science, and had advised on the establishment of a chair in physiology. But, at the banquet marking the foundation of the new buildings in 1870, he had also called on his audience not to neglect literary, historical and aesthetic studies, for 'his love of the beautiful, next to his love of the good and the true, was perhaps the greatest blessing that could be conferred on any man' (*M.G.*, 24.11.70). Four years later, opening the fine new building for the medical school, he urged Owens not to be inhibited by its formally collegiate status, for 'any corporation of men associated together for the purpose of teaching all forms of precise and accurate knowledge, the object of which was to give the highest intellectual culture that could be given, and to encourage the pursuit of knowledge in perfect freedom and without let or hindrance from any subsidiary consideration, was performing the functions of a university, and was one whatever be its name' (*ibid.*, 3.10.74).

In 1876, Huxley and his wife set out, on what they described as their 'second honeymoon', to the U.S.A., where he was to speak at the official opening of Johns Hopkins University. On hearing of the intended visit, one correspondent wrote, 'The whole nation is electrified by the news that Professor Huxley is to visit us next fall. We will make infinitely more of him than we did of the Prince of Wales and his retinue of lords and dukes' (*L.L.*, 1, 460). A century later, it is difficult to appreciate how effectively he 'electrified' audiences wherever he spoke and readers wherever his word was read. 'Any candid observer of the phenomena of modern society', he once remarked, 'will readily admit that bores must be classed among the enemies of the human race; and a little consideration will probably lead him to the further admission, that no species of that extensive genus of noxious creatures is more objectionable than the educational bore' (*C.E.*, III, 404). Whatever else he might have been, Huxley was never a bore; and his influence on educational reform was immensely aided by his pungency and wit, infused at times by a sort of pertinent irreverence which almost commanded acquiescence. As Houston Peterson has put it, 'Huxley is not only a touchstone for the last half of the nineteenth century. He is a power over us today ... He had a gift for the apt and acid phrase which reverberates after weaker words are forgotten. Huxley remains a considerable force because he happened to be a literary genius' (Peterson, vii).

Full appreciation of these qualities can come only from the cumulative effect of considerable reading, but the aroma may be savoured in a few brief selected passages. 'The modern world is full of artillery, and we turn out our children to do battle in it, equipped with the shield and sword of an ancient gladiator' (*C.E.*, VIII, 227). Or 'The State lives in a glass house; we see what it tries to do, and all its failures, partial or total, are made the most of. But private enterprise is sheltered under good opaque bricks and mortar' (*ibid.*, I, 259). Or '"Authorities", "disciples", and "schools" are the curse of science; and do more to interfere with the work of the scientific spirit than all its enemies' (*L.L.*, II, 316). Or 'it is the customary fate of new truths to begin as heresies, and to end as superstitions' (*P.R.I.*, IX, 361). Or 'I am very strongly inclined to agree with some learned schoolmasters who say that, in their experience, the teaching of science is all waste time. As they teach it, I have no doubt it is' (*C.E.*, III, 213). Or 'The besetting sin of able men is impatience of contradiction and criticism. Even those who do their best to resist the temptation, yield to it almost unconsciously and become the tools of toadies and flatterers' (*L.L.*, II, 316). Or, as a final example, 'the savage of civilisation is a more dangerous animal than any other wild beast, and . . . sooner or later every social organisation in which these ferae accumulate unduly will be torn to pieces by them' (H.P., 42.52).

But even the most apt phrases will not electrify to good effect unless they happen also to express sound sense, which almost invariably Huxley's did. At Baltimore, as in Aberdeen two years earlier, he spoke much sound sense about higher education. 'A great warrior', he reminded his audience, 'is said to have made a desert and called it peace. Administrators of educational funds have sometimes made a palace and called it a university' (*C.E.*, III, 256). He emphasised the importance of not overloading students with great masses of irrelevant detail, for 'It is impossible to say that any fragment of knowledge ... may not some day be turned to some account. But ... in order to know a little well, one must be content to be ignorant of a great deal' (*ibid.*, III, 248). And, in particular, he argued against those who used the fact of greatly increased knowledge as an excuse for crowding everything into the ordinary student's curriculum – although he did admit that 'Methuselah might, with great propriety, have taken half a century to get his doctor's degree; and might, very fairly, have been required to pass a practical examination upon the contents of the British Museum, before commencing practice as a promising young fellow of two hundred, or thereabouts' (*ibid.*, III, 221).

One of the perennial problems of education, upon which Huxley held strong views, was that of examinations. Always a realist, he had told Hooker in 1864 that the examinations of the Science and Art Department constituted 'the most important engine which has yet been invented for forcing science into ordinary Education' (H.P., 2.127). And, although he once expostulated to Michael Foster, 'It is extraordinary how those dogs of examinees return to their vomit' (*L.L.*, II, 140), he believed that properly conducted examinations had a positive rôle to play in the promotion of good teaching. For, as he later remarked of the system of 'payment by results', 'the great and manifest evil of that system ... is the steady pressure which it exerts in the development of every description of sham teaching. And the only check upon this kind of swindling the public seems to me to lie in the hands of the examiner' (*ibid.*, II, 235). So he took examinations seriously, and repeatedly emphasised that examining was a skilled occupation which required real pedagogic insight.

At University College, London, he had some scathing things to say in 1870 about the tendency of candidates to try to impress examiners by pseudo-sophisticated discussion on the basis of inadequate basic factual knowledge. 'I used to have . . . a bad reputation among students for setting up a very high standard of acquirement...', he told his audience. 'Nothing of the kind, I assure you. The defects I have noticed, and the faults I have to find, arise entirely from the circumstance that my standard is pitched too low' (*C.E.*, III, 308). Yet he was under no delusion that the same procedures as tested precision of knowledge would also provide reliable prognosis of future scholarship or research. 'In fact', he told the Aberdeen students in 1874, 'that which examination, as ordinarily conducted, tests, is simply a man's power of work under stimulus, and his capacity for rapidly and clearly producing that which, for the time, he has got into his mind. Now, these faculties are not to be despised. They are of great value in practical life... But in the pursuit of truth, scientific or other, they count for very little' (*ibid.*, III, 229). It was for this reason that in 1876 he commended to Johns Hopkins the system that he used in his own college at South Kensington, which was 'to permit the student to be examined in each subject at the end of his attendance at the class; and then, in case of the result being satisfactory, to allow him to have done with it . . . It allows the student to concentrate his mind upon what he is about for the time being, and then to dismiss it' (*ibid.*, III, 250).

When it came to examinations for a final qualification at the conclusion of a university or college course, Huxley held that they must be sufficiently severe to ensure the competence of candidates in the field which they professed.

So far as his own original subject of medicine was concerned, he remembered that, in his younger days, 'The examination might be a sham, the curriculum might be a sham, the certificate might be bought and sold like anything in a shop' (*ibid.*, III, 329). Indeed, he remarked, the system was such that 'I should think it hardly possible that it could have obtained anywhere but in such a country as England, which cherishes a fine old crusted abuse as much as it does its port wine' (*ibid.*, III, 328). However, his attitude towards examinations for entry to institutions of higher education was very different, and his feeling was distinctly against any rigidly defined entrance qualifications. Nine out of ten applicants, he believed, would meet such requirements as a mere matter of expediency, but 'I say that very possibly the odd tenth may contain persons of defective education, but of a native vigour which makes them more worth having than all the other nine-tenths, and I would not lose them for any consideration' (G.C., 563). And, he declared, 'I would make any sort of sacrifice to get rid of the Matriculation Examination. It ought not to serve the purpose of a leaving examination for the schools. What the University is now doing is to save the schools the trouble of setting up the leaving examination which they ought to have' (*ibid.*, 564). Some years later, he complained to a Select Committee that 'four-fifths of our young men are sacrificed for the minority who go to universities' (S.C.E.S.A., 1715). It all sounds remarkably relevant to issues which today are coming to the forefront of educational debate.

There were many in those days anxious to open up the universities to the middle classes, but Huxley was more concerned about opportunities for the offspring of the ordinary worker. As President of the British Association in 1870, after a drive through the streets of Liverpool in the Mayor's magnificent coach, he minced no words in

St George's Hall about 'the degradation which was worse than that of the beast' (*L.M.*, 15.11.70) in which many of the poorer citizens had to live. Nor, a few days later, did he spare another Liverpool audience some plain speaking about the existence of 'unwashed, unkempt, brutal people side by side with indications of the greatest refinement and the greatest luxury ... He did not know whether [the trade union and socialist organisations] were right or wrong, but he most heartily and profoundly sympathised with this endeavour to put down the savagery of the world' (*ibid.*, 19.11.70). He had no doubts about the intellectual potential of the working class, in which he believed that there was a vast reservoir of untapped ability. So, when in the following year he was at the peak of his activity on the London School Board, he urged that 'No one could deal with elementary education without enquiring, when he got to the end of it, What next? Was education to finish there, or was there to be a means by which persons might be able to obtain a higher education if they required it?' (*S.B.C.*, 1, 263). The financial means lay at hand in ancient charitable scholastic endowments, for 'that which was originally the birthright of the poor has been converted into a mess of pottage for distribution among the dependents of the rich' (*ibid.*, 1, 393). He succeeded in having a special committee appointed to try and get these funds applied for the benefit of pupils from the Board schools, but his health collapsed before anything much more could be achieved. He did, however, coining a phrase which was to pass into the language, advocate the establishment of 'a great educational ladder, the bottom of which shall be the gutter, and the top of which shall be the University' (*ibid.*, 1, 7).

It was not only the workers who were educationally underprivileged, and in 1860 Huxley had told Sir Charles Lyall, 'I don't see how we are to make any permanent advancement while one half of our race is sunk, as nine tenths of women are, in mere ignorant parsonese superstitions' (H.P., 30.34). As for his own daughters, he averred, 'They at any rate shall not be got up as mantraps for the matrimonial market' (*ibid.*). In 1865, when everyone was talking about the liberation of American slaves, his essay 'Emancipation – Black and White' reminded England that the female half of its own population was not yet fully freed. He openly confessed to some serious doubt whether, in view of their differing biological make-up and the heavy demands of motherhood, women were ever likely on average to match men in the highest intellectual functions; but he had no doubt at all that they should be given equal educational opportunity.

So Huxley supported Emily Davies in the establishment of Girton College for female university education, as he later did Maria Grey with her Girls' Public Day School Company and her Bishopsgate Training College for Women. In 1869, when a 'committee of ladies' sought some slight science education for their sex, he provided a course of twelve lectures which attracted over 300 auditors – and, typically mindful of their earlier educational disadvantage, went to the trouble of distributing explanatory notes in advance of each lecture. When all medical schools were closed against Elizabeth Garrett (Anderson), he admitted her to some of his classes, and soon his regular South Kensington courses were opened to students of either sex. Indeed, in 1874 he actually appointed a woman as 'demonstratrix' in Physiology. In that same year, although he was unwilling to condemn professors who refused to teach some aspects of medicine to mixed classes, he told the readers of *The Times*, 'We have heard a great deal lately about the physical disability of women. Some of these alleged impediments, no doubt, are really inherent in their organisation, but nine-tenths of them are artificial – the product of their modes of life' (*T.*, 8.7.74). And, so far as the profession of medicine was concerned, 'I am at a loss to understand on what grounds of justice or public policy a career which is open to the weakest and most foolish of the male sex should be forcibly closed to women of vigour and capacity' (*ibid.*). It is perhaps not surprising that, when the London Medical School for Women opened in the following year, it immediately applied for recognition to Aberdeen University, of which Huxley was still Rector. Nor that he told the Court, 'He himself thought the women were very hardly treated and if it depended upon him they should be examined at the University tomorrow' (*A.F.P.*, 10.5.75).

By this time much of Huxley's work for science education in the schools had already been effected. At the age of twenty-nine, speaking in St Martin's Hall 'On the Educational Value of the Natural History Sciences', he had argued for the teaching of biology to even the youngest children. 'Indeed,' he declared, 'the avidity of children for this kind of knowledge, and the comparative ease with which they retain it, is something quite marvellous' (*C.E.*, III, 64). Unlike some academics, Huxley never deluded himself that all mankind was avid for knowledge, and he knew 'what a heart-breaking business teaching is – how much the can't-learns and won't-learns and don't-learns predominate over the do-learns' (*ibid.*, VII, vii). But he also knew that everything depended upon the teacher, and repeatedly he postulated the prime conditions for successful science teaching. 'Addressing myself to you, as teachers', he said at the Science Museum in 1861, 'I would say, mere book learning in physical [natural] science is a sham and a delusion – what you teach, unless you wish to be imposters, that you must first know; and real knowledge in science means personal acquaintance with the facts' (*ibid.*, VIII, 227). Four years later, giving evidence to a

Select Committee considering the future of the 'public' schools, he remarked, first, 'that scientific teaching ... had better not be attempted at all, unless a fair share of time and attention be given to it' (S.C.P.S.B., 308); and, second, 'that the great aim should be to teach only so much science as can be taught thoroughly; and to ground in principles and methods rather than attempt to cover a large surface of details' (*ibid.*). In fact, he told the Liverpool Philomathic Society in 1869, 'If scientific education is to be dealt with as mere bookwork, it will be better not to attempt it, but to stick to the Latin Grammar which makes no pretence to be anything but bookwork' (*C.E.*, III, 125).

To counter the general belief that his ideas for science education were impracticable, Huxley arranged in 1869 to demonstrate them, before a large audience, to a class of London schoolchildren during twelve successive weeks. 'My great object', he wrote to the Reverend William Rogers, 'is to set going something which can be worked in every school in the country in a thorough and effectual way, and set an example of the manner in which I think this sort of introduction to science ought to be managed' (*L.L.*, I, 309). But, he also wrote, 'I have to stipulate ... that we shall have a clear understanding on the part of the boys and teachers that the discourses are to be *Lessons* and not talkee-talkee lectures' (*ibid.*). One eventual outcome of these lessons was that brilliant little book *Physiography*, which was still selling in substantial numbers half a century later. 'It appeared to me', Huxley wrote in the preface, 'to be plainly dictated by common sense that the teacher who wished to lead his pupils to form a clear mental picture of the order which pervades the multiform and endlessly shifting phenomena of nature, should commence with the familiar facts of the scholar's daily experience; and from the firm ground of such experience he should lead the beginner, step by step, to remoter objects and to the less readily comprehensible relations of things' (T. H. Huxley, v). And 'I do not think that a description of the earth, which commences, by telling a child that the earth is an oblate spheroid, moving round the sun in an elliptical orbit; and ends, without giving him the slightest hint towards understanding the ordnance map of his own county, or any suggestion as to the meaning of the phenomena offered by the brook which runs through his village, or the gravel pit whence the roads are mended; is calculated either to interest or to instruct' (*ibid.*, vii). This book, in fact, was the first thoroughly scientific presentation of elementary 'environmental studies' – and it is interesting that, at a much higher educational level, Patrick Geddes avowedly gained from Huxley the inspiration for his 'regional survey' method of instructing undergraduates.

Huxley did not imagine that really meaningful science education was likely to become common in schools very quickly. This, after all, was still in the period when, at Eton under Hornby, it was said that taking to drink was a much less serious offence than taking to think. At Harrow, Farrar was being obstructed in his efforts at curricular reform, so in 1867 Huxley sent him a letter of encouragement – with a characteristically shrewd sting in its tail: 'Do not despair. You are in the thick of the educational fight and must needs feel the struggle more clearly than you can see the inch by inch gain of ground – But you may depend on it victory is on your side – We or our sons shall live to see all the stupidity *in favour* of Science & I am not sure that that will not be harder to bear than the present state of things' (Farrar, 152). Twelve years later, as a Governor of Eton, he succeeded in getting properly designed laboratories built – they were still known in the 1930s as 'Huxley's Folly' – but in the meanwhile he was

4

much more concerned about the quality of science teaching in the schools of the ordinary people. So, as soon as his own new laboratories were available at South Kensington, he ran in 1871 a six-week summer school for teachers. He enrolled a class of forty-five, whose travelling and maintenance expenses were paid by the government, which also provided £100 for microscopes, £100 for materials and £520 for lecturers and demonstrators (sums which, translated into modern money values, seem to indicate powerful persuasion on Huxley's part). Soon he was writing enthusiastically to Anton Dohrn about 'a course of instruction in Biology which I am giving to Schoolmasters – with the view of converting them into scientific missionaries to convert the Christian Heathen of these islands to the true faith' (H.P., 13.202).

The following summer, despite ill-health, was spent in the same mission field; for, as Huxley told Tyndall, 'They are the commencement of a new system of teaching which, if I mistake not, will grow into a big thing and bear great fruits, and just at the present moment (nobody is necessary very long) I am the necessary man to carry it on' (ibid., 8.120). Kay-Shuttleworth evidently considered him the necessary man for a good deal longer, for in 1873 he said that 'you should be made Director for Science under the Privy Council for Education and that if you would like such a post this is the time to press for it' (ibid., 3.216). How different the development of science education might have been if Huxley had accepted this virtual invitation! But he preferred to stay in his laboratories, teaching his regular classes by that 'type system' which he invented and which was copied across half the world, to survive in many places until the present day.

One of his students has left us a vivid impression of that system in Huxley's hands: 'Though necessarily mainly anatomical and histological, it was consistently and lucidly physiological too. Taxonomy was not stressed, but clearly indicated; and the larger physiology of Nature – ecology – early opened to us in its colours and perspectives. His introduction to embryology, as at once so protean yet so deeply orderly, was never to be forgotten; and his present-ments of the palaeontological record . . . transmitted to us his clear and concrete views of their gradual evolution' (*N.*, 2897, 741). Another has sadly recorded the desiccation produced by succeeding generations of pedants: 'the original glory has departed; the great leading idea of the unity of life has been lost sight of, and the course tends to degenerate into the uninspired study of the details of structure of certain typical animals and plants' (*ibid.*, 2897, 714).

From quite early in his career, Huxley attached great importance to health education and physical education. In a lecture of 1854 he had remarked, 'were mankind deserving of the title "rational" which they arrogate to themselves, there can be no question that they would consider, as the most necessary of all branches of instruction for themselves and for their children, that which . . . teaches them how to avoid disease and to cherish health in themselves and those who are dear to them' (*C.E.*, III, 60). This interest persisted throughout his life. In 1870 he went to Liverpool to see how physical education was carried on in the Myrtle Street Gymnasium, and in the following year he served as joint secretary of the physical training section of the International Education Exhibition. A few years later he spoke at the Congress on Domestic Economy, and in 1877 he was advising Birmingham Corporation on a scheme to teach the laws of health to teachers. Soon after that he was drawing up 'a few very plain rules of health, *with reasons as far as may be*' (H.P., 29.78), for the benefit of the boys of Clifton College in Bristol. Perhaps most surprising – indeed, when one considers that the date was

1861, it is positively startling – is the nature of his teaching
of reproduction to a mixed class at Jermyn Street. 'The
first lecture', it is recorded of one female student whom
Huxley had admitted to his class, 'dealt in detail with the
physiological differences of sex, from which Elizabeth's
private tutors had shied away, and she felt the full advantage of "learning clearly and well on that very point", in
the calm atmosphere of a scientific exposition' (Manton,
122).

For Huxley, the most important of all education was
moral education, but here also he was convinced that
science had an important part to play. 'That which I mean
by "Science"', he told Kingsley in 1860, 'is not mere
physical [natural] science but all the results of exact
methods of thought whatever be the subject matter to
which they are applied ... people fancy that mathematics or physics or biology are exclusively "Science" –
and value the clothes of science more than the goddess
herself' (H.P., 19.198). He believed that 'inasmuch as the
whole universe is governed, so far as I can see, in the same
way ... the moral world is as much governed by laws as
the physical' (ibid., 19.191), and he wanted to discover
what these laws were so that mankind might live in
harmony with nature. Moral laws, of course, were not for
him platonic ideals, still less divine commands, but like
any other scientific laws were generalisations of observed
facts (in this case, of facts about the effects of differing
modes of behaviour on quality of life). 'My business', he
wrote, 'is to teach my aspirations to conform themselves
to fact, not to try and make facts harmonise with my aspirations' (ibid., 19.169). And this attitude he was prepared to
take to its logical limit: 'Even a "Traité des Passions", to
be worth anything, must be based upon observation and
experiment; and, in this subject, facilities for laboratory
practice of the most varied and extensive character were

offered by the Paris of Mazarin and the Duchesses' (*C.E.*, VI, vi).

This determinedly anti-dogmatic attitude to morality might seem to conflict with Huxley's equally determined stand for the puritan virtues of veracity, courage, assiduity and self-control, but the contradiction is largely illusory. Perhaps he exaggerated in saying, 'the longer I live, the more obvious it is to me that the most sacred act of a man's life is to say and to feel, "I believe such and such to be true"' (*H.P.*, 19.269), but he had in fact found that utter honesty enabled him to live a satisfying (because self-respecting) life. And, since the methods of science were the best provers of truth, he was genuinely prepared to accept whatever specific moral laws a thoroughly scientific investigation might disclose. That was why he once jotted down the aphorism, 'The religion which will endure is such a day dream as may still be dreamed in the noon tide glare of science' (*ibid.*, 57).

In Huxley's day there were many who opposed Darwin's theory because they considered it calculated to undermine the very bastions of morality. No doubt that is why the wife of the Bishop of Worcester, upon hearing of it, remarked to her husband, 'Descended from the apes! My dear, let us hope that it is not true, but if it is, let us pray that it will not become generally known' (Montagu, 3). On the other hand, many advocates of the cut-throat competition of unrestricted capitalism welcomed the idea of 'the struggle for existence', as providing pseudo-scientific sanction for extreme individualism. Still others took the view that careful study of the evolutionary process would provide a set of moral principles that could be considered both 'rational' and 'progressive'. Huxley regarded all three views as illusory. Of the first he once inquired, 'Is the philanthropist, or the saint, to give up his endeavours to lead a noble life, because the simplest study of man's nature reveals, at its foundations, all the selfish passions, and fierce appetites of the merest quadruped ? Is mother-love vile because a hen shews it, or fidelity base because dogs possess it ?' (*C.E.*, VII, 154). Of the second he wrote, 'society differs from nature in having a definite moral object . . . the primitive savage, or man as a mere member of the animal kingdom . . . fights out the struggle for existence to the bitter end, like any other animal . . . On the contrary, the ideal of the ethical man is to limit his freedom of action to a sphere in which he does not interfere with the freedom of others . . . which is the negation of the unlimited struggle for existence' (*ibid.*, IX, 203). As for the third, he believed that 'From the point of view of the moralist the animal world is on about the same level as a gladiator's show' (*ibid.*, IX, 199). This, of course, was the great theme of his 1893 Romanes lecture at Oxford.

Convinced as he was that 'Cosmic evolution may teach us how the good and the evil tendencies of man may have come about; but, in itself, it is incompetent to furnish any better reason why what we call good is preferable to what we call evil than we had before' (*ibid.*, IX, 80), Huxley was still left with the major philosophical problem of the ages. One could explore, and probably explain, the differences of detail between the *mores* of different societies, but why does nearly all mankind hold some things to be in principle good and others in principle bad ? He did not know the answer, and did not pretend to; but he thought that these propensities lay deep down in our biological nature and simply had to be accepted as facts. Moreover, although he was as firmly opposed to *a priori* assumptions in social or moral science as in natural science, he held that it was futile for the educator to agonise in eternal indecision. It was therefore necessary for each individual to decide as critically as possible what he believed to be right; and then, having decided, to do his best to convey his beliefs to the younger generation. And, although always immune from purblind optimism, he was opposed to anything in the nature of nihilist despair. 'This may not be the best of all possible worlds', he wrote in 1888, 'but to say that it is the worst is mere petulant nonsense. A worn-out voluptuary may find nothing good under the sun, or a vain and inexperienced youth, who cannot get the moon he cries for, may vent his irritation in pessimistic moanings, but there can be no doubt in the mind of any reasonable person that ... Men with any manhood in them find life quite worth living under worse conditions than these' (*ibid.*, IX, 201). Somehow it all sounds extremely relevant to some contemporary campus debates.

As in his middle and later years he became a great power in the land, Huxley increasingly applied his educational efforts to administration and to national policy. When in 1870 most of the senior professors concerned were opposed to the government's (and Huxley's) plan for a major central school of science at South Kensington, he used every ounce of political skill to bring biology, chemistry, physics, geology, metallurgy and mining under the one roof. And, although *de jure* he held no special position there, this did not prevent his acting virtually as *de facto* head of the combined institution. But he wanted to go further, for he was convinced that it was absurd to leave the production of science teachers to the church-dominated training colleges, where 'Half the time of their students is occupied with grinding into their minds their tweedle-dum and tweedle-dee theological idiocies, and the other half in cramming them with boluses of other things to be duly spat out on examination day' (*L.L.*, II, 156). By 1881 he had his way, with South Kensington redesignated as a Normal School of Science and himself at its head as Dean. This title not only amused his agnostic friends, but sufficiently misled the mother of young H. G. Wells to permit his attendance as a student despite the horrendous things she had heard about Huxley.

During his first year as Dean, the School's library and museum were reorganised, research facilities were provided free of charge for students of proved ability, and the associateship diploma was opened to women. Before long the lecturing staff were prohibited from accepting private payments either for scientific investigations conducted on the premises for industrial concerns, or for private tuition of students. And soon Huxley's long-advocated scheme of instruction, with all students taking a common science course during the first year and only electing specialisms in the second, was adopted. When, in 1885, he resigned his professorial chair, the government persuaded him to continue as Honorary Dean, which he did until his death a decade later.

Concurrently with his daily work at South Kensington, Huxley became deeply involved in the promotion of technical education. In 1868 he had already declared, 'first, that England was no longer the premier power of nations; secondly, that though this was true it didn't matter. For though we might never again be so great in the scale of nationalities, we might become a greater nation, by each individual using to the utmost the faculties bestowed upon him' (*S.L.P.*, 7.3.78). But he did not believe that any narrow sort of scientific or technical instruction could possibly provide an adequate answer to the challenge of the times. 'Many people', he pointed out in 1871, 'thought they had only to have a school for science, and that everything would be done that was needful, that manufactures would flourish henceforth, and that this was the one thing needful: but he believed that to be a profound and mischievous mistake' (*S.B.C.*, ii, 263). And, he said at the Society of Arts in 1879, 'Although it was a great thing to make skilled workmen, yet it was much more important to make intelligent men' (N., XXI, 139). So, taking the term 'technical education' to cover 'all those means by which the productive capacity of an industrial population may be fully and permanently developed' (H.P., 42.58), he did everything in his power to promote general educational and recreational facilities. He believed that there was a real reciprocal relationship between material advancement and social morality, for 'Becky Sharp's acute remark, that it is not difficult to be virtuous on ten thousand a year, has its application to nations; and it is futile to expect a hungry and squalid population to be anything but violent and gross' (C.E., III, 33). And, from the other side of this relationship, he urged the Charity Commissioners to provide 'baths, gymnasia, cookery schools, free libraries, reading rooms & innocent amusements as a contribution to industrial development of prime importance' (H.P., 42.52).

Huxley had been extremely impressed by the vigorous manner in which some northern towns had tackled the problem of technical education, and especially noted that a little place like Keighley had managed to provide its local institute with equipment to the tune of nearly £20,000. In London, on the other hand, there were great city companies and guilds which had done very little in this field. It is noticeable how frequently, from about 1870, Huxley began to attend Mansion House banquets, and it is not difficult to guess how a good deal of his conversation was directed. From about 1875 he was *persona gratissima* to the Livery, despite the alternate advice and cajolery to which he subjected them. In the December of 1879 he publicly reminded the companies that they 'possessed enormous wealth, which had been left to them for the benefit of the trades they represent . . . that they were morally bound to do this work, and he hoped if they continued to neglect the obligation they would be legally compelled to do it' (N., XXI, 139). Continuing his campaign in the columns of

The Times, he complained that 'The inmost financial secrets of the Church and of the colleges of Oxford and Cambridge have been laid bare by those universal solvents, Royal Commissions; but no Government which has existed in this country for the last century has been strong enough to apply such *aqua regia* to the strong-boxes of the City Guilds' (*T.*, 15.12.79). By January 1880 he was telling a friend, 'The animal is moving and by a judicious combination of carrots in front and kicks behind, we shall get him into a fine trot presently' (*L.L.*, 1, 476).

The companies quickly provided the money to build a fine new technical college in Finsbury, which opened in 1883. The following year saw the establishment of the City and Guilds College in South Kensington. 'I think you must admit that the City companies have yielded liberally to the gentle compression you have exercised on them' (H.P., 12.107), a leading liveryman wrote to Huxley. It was with some legitimate pride that, addressing the Royal Society as its President in 1885, Huxley announced that already there were some 250 technical classes affiliated to the City and Guilds of London Institute – of which, according to one of its most important members, Huxley was 'really the engineer ... for without his advice we should not have known what to have done' (*L.L.*, 1, 474).

During the nine years between returning from Baltimore and resigning his professorial chair at South Kensington, Huxley continued to receive honours from overseas institutions, including the Academia de' Lincei of Rome, the Dutch Academy of Sciences, the Academy of Letters of Pernambuco, the Royal Society of New South Wales, the Institute de France and the Geological Society of Australasia. Still unable to deny requests for voluntary public service, he became a member of three more Royal Commissions, a Crown Senator of London University, a Trustee of the British Museum, Vice-President of the

Society of Authors and of the Working Men's Club and
Institute Union, a Governor of Eton and President of the
Royal Society. During these same years his eldest son
Leonard went first to St Andrews and then to Oxford,
Marian had her first painting hung by the Royal Academy
and Ethel won a prize for modelling at the Slade School,
while Jessie and Marian and Rachel all married. In 1878
Huxley wrote the bulk of his book *Hume* during a six-
week holiday at Penmaenmawr, and taught himself Greek
so as to read Aristotle in the original. In 1879 he received
another honorary doctorate, telling a friend, 'I shall be
glorious in a red gown at Cambridge tomorrow, and hereafter look to be treated as a PERSON OF RESPECTABILITY. I
have done my best to avoid that misfortune, but it's of
no use!' (*L.L.*, II, 4). In 1881 he was sorely tempted by two
virtual invitations from Oxford, first to the Linacre Chair
and then to the Master's Lodge of University College, but
finally turned them both down – telling his son Leonard,
'I do not think I am cut out for a Don nor your mother for
a Donness' (*ibid.*, II, 32). The following year he rejected a
rich offer from Harvard of $10,000 per annum 'for the
benefit of your presence and influence' (H.P., 6.146). In
1884 he began a slight disengagement from public affairs
by resigning his Presidency of the National Association of
Science Teachers. But – characteristically – in 1885 he
put yet another iron in the fire by beginning his ebullient
controversy with Gladstone about the conflict between
geology and Genesis.

Huxley's health at the time of his retirement was so
precarious that he was not expected to last very long, but
fortunately things did not turn out quite like that. Conva-
lescent visits to Switzerland aroused a new scientific interest
in the hybridism and phylogeny of gentians, together with a
devotion to alpines in general which was applied in his
retirement hobby of gardening. He conspired with Jowett

of Balliol to bring about reforms in medicine at Oxford, but they had only partial success in relieving science students of compulsory classical language requirements. With greater leisure, Huxley was seen more often at meetings of the Literary and Dickens and Rabelais Societies; and in 1886 he made a powerful public protest against the neglect of literary studies at Oxford. 'That a young Englishman may be turned out of one of our universities, "epopt and perfect" so far as their system takes him, and yet ignorant of the noble literature which has grown up in these islands during the last three centuries...', he declared, 'is a fact in the history of the nineteenth century which the twentieth will find hard to believe' (*P.M.G.*, 22.10.86). In 1887 Huxley gave up most of his examining, but before very long began his extended public controversy on the still somewhat scandalous subject of agnosticism. In 1888 he accepted the Presidency of the International Geological Congress, but in the following year moved to Eastbourne in an attempt (not, as it turned out, too successful) at cutting completely free from the society and societies of London. Meanwhile, his darling daughter Marian had died a tragic death, Leonard and Nettie and Harry had contracted quite orthodox marriages, and Huxley had taken Ethel to Norway for a wedding with Marian's widower in defiance of England's law against marriage to a deceased wife's sister. In 1892, having previously declined on principle the offer of a peerage, he accepted membership of the Privy Council since that was an office and not an honour. 'The Archbishopric of Canterbury is the only object of ambition that remains to me', he told Hooker. 'Come and be Suffragan; there is plenty of room at Lambeth and a capital garden!' (H.P., 2.419).

Huxley had long held that there should be a clear national policy coordinating professional, higher technical and general university education; and he saw no reason why the award of degrees should be confined to the traditional faculties. As early as 1869, for example, he had suggested that the London teacher-training colleges should be federated under a dean, that the provincial colleges should be similarly federated and that there should be an 'Examining body for the whole formed by selection from the professors of all the Colleges ... not to be called a University – National Institute – Degrees granted by Minister on recommendation of Examiners' (*ibid.*, 42.194). In 1884 he had recommended, against the whole anti-State feeling of the time, that there should be an 'influential Minister, with a seat in the Cabinet, enabling him to give the greatest force to his views which a Minister can give ... to judge the direction in which the educational necessities of the times are tending ... by distinct regulation occasionally, if necessary, to force ... a modification ... in the desired direction' (S.C.E.S.A., 1737) – but, he added, 'not to interfere and reduce the whole educational system of the country to one dead level' (*ibid.*, 1748). In 1886 he was appointed to a special committee of the London University Senate, where he tried to get medical graduating rights granted to the professional colleges, and where he sought also to bring London's legal education bodies into close relationship. In 1887 he urged that the projected Imperial (now Commonwealth) Institute should be placed not at South Kensington but in the City, where it might become 'a place ... in which the higher questions of commerce and industry would be systematically studied and elucidated; and where, as in an industrial university, the whole technical education of the country might find its centre and crown' (*T.*, 20.1.87).

But none of these very forward-looking plans secured general or complete acceptance. Throughout the 1880s, all efforts at introducing some order and coherent pattern into the higher education of the metropolis foundered in the rough seas of fundamentally differing opinions and opposing partisan interests. Some wanted the colleges to be absorbed by the university; some wanted them to grant their own degrees; some wanted a loose federation. Many favoured the handing over of all power to the professors; many others would have given a good deal to the general body of graduates; a smaller but strong group would have kept important reserve powers for the college principals. The air became thick with schemes and counter-schemes, with petitions to Privy Council and the like. The government tried to settle matters by appointing first the 1888 Selborne Commission and then the 1892 Cowper ('Gresham') Commission, but to no avail. Things in London looked remarkably like the national picture of higher education today. By the spring of 1892 Huxley had given up hope of any valuable outcome, and lamented to Sir John Donnelly that 'The whole affair is a perfect muddle of competing crude projects and vested interests, and is likely to end in a worse muddle' (L.L., II, 311). To Lankester he wrote, 'unless people clearly understand that the university of the future is to be a very different thing from the university of the past, they had better put off meddling for another generation' (H.P., 30.143). And, so far as efforts to absorb his own South Kensington School into the existing university were concerned, he warned, 'I am ready to oppose any such project tooth and nail. I have not been striving these thirty years to get Science clear of their schoolmastering sham-literary peddling to give up the game without a fight' (L.L., II, 312).

Then, quite suddenly, a vigorous group of younger men led by Karl Pearson began to organise effectively, and before midsummer Huxley was back in the fray. 'I . . . have told the rising generation that this old hulk is ready to be towed out into line of battle', he informed Michael Foster, 'which is more commendable to my public spirit than my prudence' (*ibid.*, II, 333). Almost immediately he became President of the new Association, and Pearson (who wanted a constitution on Germanic lines) found himself hopelessly out-manoeuvred. 'As for a government by professors only', Huxley wrote to *The Times*, 'the fact of their being specialists is against them. Most of them are broadminded, practical men; some are good administrators. But, unfortunately, there is among them, as in other professions, a fair sprinkling of one-idea'd fanatics, ignorant of the commonest conventions of official relations, and content with nothing if they cannot get their own way. It is these persons who, with the very highest and purest intentions, would ruin any administrative body unless they were counterpoised by non-professorial, common-sense members of recognised weight and authority in the conduct of affairs' (*T.*, 6.12.92). He started attending again at university committee meetings, and was soon writing to his son-in-law John Collier, 'You should see the place I am claiming for Art in the University. I do believe something will grow out of my plan, which has made all the dry bones rattle . . . I shall be coming to you to have my wounds dressed after the fight' (*L.L.*, II, 307). He was enjoying himself more than for many a year.

Huxley's plan, which is preserved in detail on nine foolscap sheets, was one of extraordinary interest. The metropolitan university was to be formed from sub-federations of 'Institutions giving instruction for purposes of: i. General Education (Arts). ii. Professional education in (a) Law (b) Medicine (c) The Industrial Professions (d) The Scholastic Profession (e) Painting, Sculpture and Architecture (f) Music. iii. Research in any of the Schools' (H.P., 42.110). The federation of General Education institutions was to include the non-professional faculties of University College, King's College, etc; and was to be responsible for the extension teaching of adults who could study only part-time but wished to take university examinations. The several sub-federations of Professional Education (which would also include the training of clergy if the denominations could reach agreement) were to be semi-autonomous, arranging their own curricula and degree examinations. The Research sub-federation was to include both purely research institutions and the major research departments of the teaching colleges and faculties. Cutting right across these federations there was to be a series of schools, each consisting of the teachers in a prescribed range of disciplines, irrespective of whether they worked in a traditional faculty, a professional college or a research institution. And, out of the teachers of the appropriate schools, Senate was to constitute Boards of Studies for the many subjects studied somewhere in the university. Today, no doubt, this would be described as a blue-print for a 'comprehensive university'. Of course, Huxley's plan was not adopted in anything like its full richness, but enough of it took hold for him to head a united delegation to the Prime Minister in December 1894, to speak for all the interests involved, and thus to clear the way for the great new federal University of London.

Six months later, after a lifetime of personal liveliness and family warmth and almost unremitting scientific and educational effort, Thomas Henry Huxley died peacefully at Eastbourne on 29 June 1895. 'Posthumous fame is not particularly attractive to me', he had told the old Chartist George Howell, 'but, if I am to be remembered at all, I would rather it should be as "a man who did his best to help the people" than by any other title' (*L.L.*, 1, 476). He was buried at Finchley, without religious ceremony.

ON THE EDUCATIONAL VALUE OF THE
NATURAL HISTORY SCIENCES

(1854)

Science is, I believe, nothing but *trained and organised common sense*, differing from the latter only as a veteran may differ from a raw recruit: and its methods differ from those of common sense only so far as the guardsman's cut and thrust differ from the manner in which a savage wields his club. The primary power is the same in each case, and perhaps the untutored savage has the more brawny arm of the two. The *real* advantage lies in the point and polish of the swordsman's weapon; in the trained eye quick to spy out the weakness of the adversary; in the ready hand prompt to follow it on the instant. But, after all, the sword exercise is only the hewing and poking of the clubman developed and perfected.

So, the vast results obtained by Science are won by no mystical faculties, by no mental processes, other than those which are practised by every one of us, in the humblest and meanest affairs of life. A detective policeman discovers a burglar from the marks made by his shoe, by a mental process identical with that by which Cuvier restored the extinct animals of Montmartre from fragments of their bones. Nor does that process of induction and deduction by which a lady, finding a stain of a peculiar kind upon her dress, concludes that somebody has upset the inkstand thereon, differ in any way, in kind, from that by which Adams and Leverrier discovered a new planet.

The man of science, in fact, simply uses with scrupulous exactness the methods which we all, habitually and at every moment, use carelessly ... If, however, there be no real difference between the methods of science and those of common life, it would seem, on the face of the matter, highly improbable that there should be any difference between the methods of the different sciences; nevertheless, it is constantly taken for granted that there is a very wide difference between the Physiological [Biological] and other sciences in point of method. . . .

No such differences, I believe, really exist. The subject-matter . . . is different . . . but the methods of all are identical; and these methods are –

1. *Observation* of facts – including under this head that *artificial observation* which is called *experiment*.

2. That process of tying up similar facts into bundles, ticketed and ready for use, which is called *Comparison* and *Classification* – the results of the process, the ticketed bundles, being named *General propositions*.

3. *Deduction*, which takes us from the general proposition to facts again – teaches us, if I may so say, to anticipate from the ticket what is inside the bundle. And finally –

4. *Verification*, which is the process of ascertaining whether, in point of fact, our anticipation is a correct one. Such are the methods of all science whatsoever . . .

But as the student, in reaching Biology, looks back upon sciences of a less complex and therefore more perfect nature; so, on the other hand, does he look forward to other more complex and less perfect branches of knowledge . . . There is a higher division of science still, which . . . *observes* men – whose *experiments* are made by nations one upon another, in battlefields – whose *general propositions* are embodied in history, morality, and religion – whose *deductions* lead to our happiness or our misery – and whose *verifications* so often come too late, and serve only

To point a moral, or adorn a tale –

I mean the science of Society or *Sociology*.

I think it is one of the grandest features of Biology, that it occupies this central position in human knowledge. There is no side of the human mind which physiological study leaves uncultivated. Connected by innumerable ties with abstract science, Physiology is yet in the most intimate relation with humanity; and by teaching us that law and order, and a definite scheme of development, regulate even the strangest and wildest manifestations of individual life, she prepares the student to look for a goal even amidst the erratic wanderings of mankind, and to believe that history offers something more than an entertaining chaos – a journal of a toilsome, tragi-comic march nowhither . . .

Its [Biology's] *subject-matter* is a large moiety of the universe – its *position* is midway between the physico-chemical and the social sciences. Its *value* as a branch of discipline is partly that which it has in common with all sciences – the training and strengthening of common sense; partly that which is more peculiar to itself – the great exercise which it affords to the faculties of observation and comparison; and, I may add, the *exactness* of knowledge which it requires on the part of those among its votaries who desire to extend its boundaries . . .

[The question –] What is the practical value of physiological instruction? – might, one would think, be left to answer itself . . . Why is it that educated men can be found to maintain that a slaughter-house in the midst of a great city is rather a good thing than otherwise? – that mothers persist in exposing the largest possible amount of surface of their children to the cold . . . and then marvel at the peculiar dispensation of Providence, which removes their infants by bronchitis and gastric fever? Why is it that quackery rides rampant over the land? . . . Why is all this, except from the utter ignorance as to the simplest laws of their own animal life, which prevails among even the most highly educated persons in this country? . . .

There is yet another way in which natural history may, I am convinced, take a profound hold upon practical life – and that is, by its influence over our finer feelings, as the greatest of all sources of that pleasure which is derivable from beauty. I do not pretend that natural-history knowledge, as such, can increase our sense of the beautiful in natural objects. I do not suppose that the dead soul of Peter Bell, of whom the great poet of nature says, –

> A primrose by the river's brim,
> A yellow primrose was to him, –
> And it was nothing more, –

would have been a whit roused from its apathy by the information that the primrose is a Dicotyledonous Exogen, with a monopetalous corolla and central placentation. But I advocate natural-history knowledge from this point of view, because it would lead us to *seek* the beauties of natural objects, instead of trusting to chance to force them on our attention. To a person uninstructed in natural history, his country or sea-side stroll is a walk through a gallery filled with wonderful works of art, nine-tenths of which have their faces turned to the wall. Teach him something of natural history, and you place in his hands a catalogue of those which are worth turning round . . .

Biology needs no apologist when she demands a place – and a prominent place – in any scheme of education worthy of the name. Leave out the Physiological sciences from your curriculum, and you launch the student into the world, undisciplined in that science whose subject-matter would best develop his powers of observation; ignorant of facts of the deepest importance for his own and others' welfare; blind to the richest sources of beauty in God's creation; and unprovided with that belief in a living law, and an order manifesting itself in and through endless change and variety, which might serve to check and moderate that phase of despair through which, if he take an earnest interest in social problems, he will assuredly sooner or later pass...

Collected Essays, III, 38–65

Address at Society of Arts' educational exhibition, St Martin's Hall, Long Acre (under the title 'On the Relation of Physiological Science to Other Branches of Knowledge'), 22 July 1854

Summary in *Journal of Society of Arts*, II (28 July 1854), 625

Published in full as pamphlet (Van Voorst (London), 1854)

Reprinted in T. H. Huxley, *Lay Sermons, Addresses and Reviews* (Macmillan, 1870)

A LOBSTER;
OR, THE STUDY OF ZOOLOGY

(1861)

There is not a fragment of the organism of this humble
animal whose study would not lead us into [large] regions
of thought ... The great matter is, to make teaching real
and practical, by fixing the attention of the student on
particular facts; but at the same time it should be rendered
broad and comprehensive, by constant reference to the
generalisations of which all particular facts are illustrations.
The lobster has served as a type of the whole animal kingdom, and its anatomy and physiology have illustrated for
us some of the greatest truths of biology. The student who
has once seen for himself the facts which I have described,
has had their relations explained to him, and has clearly
comprehended them, has, so far, a knowledge of zoology,
which is real and genuine, however limited it may be, and
which is worth more than all the mere reading knowledge
of the science he could ever acquire ...

The object of lectures is, in the first place, to awaken
the attention and excite the enthusiasm of the student; and
this, I am sure, may be effected to a far greater extent by
the oral discourse and by the personal influence of a
respected teacher than in any other way. Secondly, lectures
have the double use of guiding the student to the salient
points of a subject, and at the same time forcing him to
attend to the whole of it, and not merely to that part which
takes his fancy. And lastly, lectures afford the student the
opportunity of seeking explanations of those difficulties
which will, and indeed ought to, arise in the course of his
studies ...

A properly composed course of lectures ought to contain fully as much matter as a student can assimilate in the time occupied by its delivery; and the teacher should always recollect that his business is to feed, and not to cram the intellect. Indeed, I believe that a student who gains from a course of lectures the simple habit of concentrating his attention upon a definitely limited series of facts, until they are thoroughly mastered, has made a step of immeasurable importance.

But, however good lectures may be, and however extensive the course of reading by which they are followed up, they are but accessories to the great instrument of scientific teaching – demonstration. If I insist unweariedly, nay fanatically, upon the importance of physical science as an educational agent, it is because the study of any branch of science, if properly conducted, appears to me to fill up a void left by all other means of education. I have the greatest respect and love for literature; nothing would grieve me more than to see literary training other than a very prominent branch of education: indeed, I wish that real literary discipline were far more attended to than it is; but I cannot shut my eyes to the fact, that there is a vast difference between men who have had a purely literary, and those who have had a sound scientific, training.

Seeking for the cause of this difference, I imagine I can find it in the fact that, in the world of letters, learning and knowledge are one, and books are the source of both; whereas in science, as in life, learning and knowledge are distinct, and the study of things, and not of books, is the source of the latter.

All that literature has to bestow may be obtained by reading and by practical exercise in writing and in speaking; but I do not exaggerate when I say, that none of the best gifts of science are to be won by these means. On the contrary, the great benefit which a scientific education bestows, whether as training or as knowledge, is dependent upon the extent to which the mind of the student is brought into immediate contact with facts – upon the degree to which he learns the habit of appealing directly to Nature, and of acquiring through his senses concrete images of those properties of things, which are, and always will be, but approximatively expressed in human language. Our way of looking at Nature, and of speaking about her, varies from year to year; but a fact once seen, a relation of cause and effect, once demonstratively apprehended, are possessions which neither change nor pass away, but, on the contrary, form fixed centres, about which other truths aggregate by natural affinity.

Therefore, the great business of the scientific teacher is, to imprint the fundamental, irrefragable facts of his science, not only by words upon the mind, but by sensible impression upon the eye, and ear, and touch of the student, in so complete a manner, that every term used, or law enunciated, should afterwards call up vivid images of the particular structural, or other, facts which furnished the demonstration of the law, or the illustration of the term.

Now this important operation can only be achieved by constant demonstration, which may take place to a certain imperfect extent during a lecture, but which ought also to be carried on independently, and which should be addressed to each individual student, the teacher endeavouring, not so much to show a thing to the learner, as to make him see it for himself.

I am well aware that there are great practical difficulties in the way of effectual zoological demonstrations. The dissection of animals is not altogether pleasant, and requires much time; nor is it easy to secure an adequate supply of the needful specimens . . .

A good deal may be done, however, without actual dissection on the student's part, by demonstration upon specimens and preparations; and in all probability it would not be very difficult, were the demand sufficient, to organise collections of such objects, sufficient for all the purposes of elementary teaching, at a comparatively cheap rate. Even without these, much might be effected, if the zoological collections, which are open to the public, were arranged according to what has been termed the 'typical principle'; that is to say, if the specimens exposed to public view were so selected that the public could learn something from them, instead of being, as at present, merely confused by their multiplicity. For example, the grand ornithological gallery at the British Museum contains between two and three thousand species of birds, and sometimes five or six specimens of a species. They are very pretty to look at, and some of the cases are, indeed, splendid; but I will undertake to say, that no man but a professional orni-thologist has ever gathered much information from the collection. Certainly, no one of the tens of thousands of the general public who have walked through that gallery ever knew more about the essential peculiarities of birds when he left the gallery than when he entered it. But if, somewhere in that vast hall, there were a few preparations, exemplifying the leading structural peculiarities and the mode of development of a common fowl; if the types of the genera, the leading modifications in the skeleton, in the plumage at various ages, in the mode of nidification, and the like, among birds, were displayed; and if the other specimens were put away in a place where the men of science, to whom they are alone useful, could have free access to them, I can conceive that this collection might become a great instrument of scientific education.

The last implement of the teacher ... is examina-tion ... I hold that both written and oral examinations are indispensable ...

But there ... is the question, why should teachers be

encouraged to acquire a knowledge of [zoology], or any other branch of physical [natural] science? What is the use, it is said, of attempting to make physical science a branch of primary education? Is it not probable that teachers, in pursuing such studies, will be led astray from the acquirement of more important but less attractive knowledge? And, even if they can learn something of science without prejudice to their usefulness, what is the good of attempting to instil that knowledge into boys whose real business is the acquisition of reading, writing, and arithmetic?

These questions are, and will be, very commonly asked, for they arise from that profound ignorance of the value and true position of physical science, which infests the minds of the most highly educated and intelligent classes of the community. But if I did not feel well assured that they are capable of being easily and satisfactorily answered; that they have been answered over and over again; and that the time will come when men of liberal education will blush to raise such questions – I should be ashamed of my position here to-night. Without doubt, it is your great and very important function to carry out elementary education; without question, anything that should inter-fere with the faithful fulfilment of that duty on your part would be a great evil; and if I thought that your acquire-ment of the elements of physical science, and your com-munication of those elements to your pupils, involved any sort of interference with your proper duties, I should be the first person to protest against your being encouraged to do anything of the kind.

But is it true that the acquisition of such a knowledge of science as is proposed, and the communication of that knowledge, are calculated to weaken your usefulness? Or may I not rather ask, is it possible for you to discharge your functions properly without these aids?

What is the purpose of primary intellectual education ? I apprehend that its first object is to train the young in the use of those tools wherewith men extract knowledge from the ever-shifting succession of phenomena which pass before their eyes; and that its second object is to inform them of the fundamental laws which have been found by experience to govern the course of things, so that they may not be turned out into the world naked, defenceless, and a prey to the events they might control.

A boy is taught to read his own and other languages, in order that he may have access to infinitely wider stores of knowledge than could ever be opened to him by oral intercourse with his fellow men; he learns to write, that his means of communication with the rest of mankind may be indefinitely enlarged, and that he may record and store up the knowledge he acquires. He is taught elementary mathematics, that he may understand all those relations of number and form, upon which the transactions of men, associated in complicated societies, are built, and that he may have some practice in deductive reasoning.

All these operations of reading, writing, and ciphering, are intellectual tools, whose use should, before all things, be learned, and learned thoroughly; so that the youth may be enabled to make his life that which it ought to be, a continual progress in learning and in wisdom.

But, in addition, primary education endeavours to fit a boy out with a certain equipment of positive knowledge. He is taught the great laws of morality; the religion of his sect; so much history and geography as will tell him where the great countries of the world are, what they are, and how they have become what they are.

Without doubt all these are most fitting and excellent things to teach a boy; I should be very sorry to omit any of them from any scheme of primary intellectual education. The system is excellent, so far as it goes.

But if I regard it closely, a curious reflection arises. I suppose that, fifteen hundred years ago, the child of any well-to-do Roman citizen was taught just these same things; reading and writing in his own, and, perhaps, the Greek tongue; the elements of mathematics; and the religion, morality, history, and geography current in his time. Furthermore, I do not think I err in affirming that, if such a Christian Roman boy, who had finished his education, could be transplanted into one of our public schools, and pass through its course of instruction, he would not meet with a single unfamiliar line of thought; amidst all the new facts he would have to learn, not one would suggest a different mode of regarding the universe from that current in his own time.

And yet surely there is some great difference between the civilisation of the fourth century and that of the nineteenth, and still more between the intellectual habits and tone of thought of that day and this?

And what has made this difference? I answer fearlessly – The prodigious development of physical science within the last two centuries.

Modern civilisation rests upon physical science; take away her gifts to our own country, and our position among the leading nations of the world is gone to-morrow; for it is physical science only that makes intelligence and moral energy stronger than brute force.

The whole of modern thought is steeped in science; it has made its way into the works of our best poets, and even the mere man of letters, who affects to ignore and despise science, is unconsciously impregnated with her spirit, and indebted for his best products to her methods. I believe that the greatest intellectual revolution mankind has yet seen is now slowly taking place by her agency. She is teaching the world that the ultimate court of appeal is observation and experiment, and not authority; she is teaching it to estimate the value of evidence; she is creating a firm and living faith in the existence of immutable moral and physical laws, perfect obedience to which is the highest possible aim of an intelligent being.

But of all this your old stereotyped system of education takes no note. Physical science, its methods, its problems, and its difficulties, will meet the poorest boy at every turn, and yet we educate him in such a manner that he shall enter the world as ignorant of the existence of the methods and facts of science as the day he was born. The modern world is full of artillery; and we turn out our children to do battle in it, equipped with the shield and sword of an ancient gladiator.

Posterity will cry shame on us if we do not remedy this deplorable state of things. Nay, if we live twenty years longer, our own consciences will cry shame on us.

It is my firm conviction that the only way to remedy it is to make the elements of physical science an integral part of primary education. I have endeavoured to show you how that may be done for that branch of science which it is my business to pursue; and I can but add, that I should look upon the day when every schoolmaster throughout this land was a centre of genuine, however rudimentary, scientific knowledge, as an epoch in the history of the country . . .

Collected Essays, VIII, 196–228

Address at South Kensington Museum (under the title 'On the Study of Zoology'), 1861

Published as pamphlet by Department of Science and Art (1861)

Reprinted in T. H. Huxley, *Lay Sermons, Addresses and Reviews* (Macmillan, 1870)

EMANCIPATION – BLACK AND WHITE
(1865)

The doctrine of equal natural rights may be an illogical delusion; emancipation may convert the slave from a well-fed animal into a pauperised man; mankind may even have to do without cotton shirts; but all these evils must be faced if the moral law, that no human being can arbitrarily dominate over another without grievous damage to his own nature, be, as many think, as readily demonstrable by experiment as any physical truth . . .

The like considerations apply to all the other questions of emancipation which are at present stirring the world . . . One of the most important, if not the most important, of all these, is . . . What social and political rights have women ? What ought they to be allowed, or not allowed, to do, be, and suffer ? And, as involved in, and underlying all these questions, how ought they to be educated ?

There are philogynists as fanatical as any 'misogynists' who, reversing our antiquated notions, bid the man look upon the woman as the higher type of humanity; who ask us to regard the female intellect as the clearer and the quicker, if not the stronger; who desire us to look up to the feminine moral sense as the purer and the nobler; and bid man abdicate his usurped sovereignty over Nature in favour of the female line. On the other hand, there are persons . . . by nature hard of head and haters of delusion . . . who not only repudiate the new woman-worship . . . but . . . deny even the natural equality of the sexes . . . Tell these persons of the rapid perceptions and the instinctive intellectual insight of women, and they reply that the feminine mental peculiarities . . . are merely the outcome of a greater impressibility to the superficial aspects of things, and of the absence of ... restraint upon expression ... Talk of the passive endurance of the weaker sex, and opponents of this kind remind you that Job was a man ... Claim passionate tenderness as especially feminine, and the inquiry is made whether all the best love-poetry in existence (except, perhaps, the 'Sonnets from the Portuguese') has not been written by men ...

Supposing, however, that all these arguments have a certain foundation ... Granting the alleged defects of women, is it not somewhat absurd to sanction and maintain a system of education which would seem to have been specially contrived to exaggerate all these defects ?

Naturally not so firmly strung, nor so well balanced as boys, girls are in great measure debarred from .. sports and physical exercises ... Women are, by nature, more excitable than men – prone to be swept by tides of emotion ... and female education does its best to ... stimulate the emotional part of the mind and stunt the rest. We find girls naturally timid, inclined to dependence, born conservatives; and we teach them that independence is unladylike; that blind faith is the right frame of mind; and that ... our sister is to be left to the tyranny of authority and tradition. With few insignificant exceptions, girls have been educated either to be drudges, or toys, beneath man; or a sort of angels above him ... The possibility that the ideal of womanhood lies neither in the fair saint, nor in the fair sinner; that the female type of character is neither better nor worse than the male, but only weaker; that women are meant neither to be men's guides nor their playthings, but their comrades, their fellows, and their equals, so far as Nature puts no bar to that equality, does not seem to have entered into the minds of those who have had the conduct of the education of girls.

If the present system of female education stands self-condemned, as inherently absurd ... what is the first step towards a better state of things ? We reply, emancipate girls. Recognise the fact that they share the senses, perceptions, feelings, reasoning powers, emotions, of boys, and that the mind of the average girl is less different from that of the average boy, than the mind of one boy is from that of another; so that whatever argument justifies a given education for all boys, justifies its application to girls as well. So far from imposing artificial restrictions upon the acquirement of knowledge by women, throw every facility in their way. Let our Faustinas, if they will, toil through the whole round of

> Juristerei und Medizin,
> Und leider! auch Philosophie.

Let us have 'sweet girl graduates' by all means. They will be none the less sweet for a little wisdom; and the 'golden hair' will not curl less gracefully outside the head by reason of there being brains within. Nay, if obvious practical difficulties can be overcome, let those women who feel inclined to do so descend into the gladiatorial arena of life ... Let them, if they so please, become merchants, barristers, politicians. Let them have a fair field, but let them understand, as the necessary correlative, that they are to have no favour ...

And the result ? For our part, though loth to prophesy, we believe it will be that of other emancipations. Women will find their place, and it will neither be that in which they have been held, nor that to which some of them aspire. Nature's old salique law will not be repealed, and no change of dynasty will be effected. The big chests, the massive brains, the vigorous muscles and stout frames of the best men will carry the day, whenever it is worth their while to contest the prizes of life with the best women ...

We are, indeed, fully prepared to believe that the bearing of children may, and ought, to become as free from danger and long disability to the civilised woman as it is to the savage; nor is it improbable that, as society advances towards its right organisation, motherhood will occupy a less space of woman's life than it has hitherto done. But still, unless the human species is to come to an end altogether ... somebody must be good enough to take the trouble and responsibility of annually adding to the world exactly as many people as die out of it ... And we fear that so long as this potential motherhood is her lot, woman will be found to be fearfully weighted in the race of life.

The duty of man is to see that not a grain is piled upon that load beyond what Nature imposes; that injustice is not added to inequality.

Collected Essays, III, 66–75
Published in *The Reader* (20 May 1865)
Reprinted in T. H. Huxley, *Lay Sermons, Addresses and Reviews* (Macmillan, 1870)

ON THE ADVISABLENESS OF
IMPROVING NATURAL KNOWLEDGE

(1866)

This time two hundred years ago – in the beginning of January 1666 – those of our forefathers who inhabited this great and ancient city, took breath between the shocks of two fearful calamities . . .

They submitted to the plague in humility and in penitence, for they believed it to be the judgment of God. But, towards the fire they were furiously indignant, interpreting it as the effect of the malice of man, – as the work of the Republicans, or of the Papists . . . It would, I fancy, have fared but ill with one who . . . should have broached to our ancestors the doctrine which I now propound to you – that all their hypotheses were alike wrong . . . that they were themselves authors of both plague and fire, and that they must look to themselves to prevent the recurrence of [such] calamities . . .

Some twenty years before the outbreak of the plague a few calm and thoughtful students banded themselves together . . . [and founded what became] the 'Royal Society for the Improvement of Natural Knowledge' . . . It is very certain that for every victim slain by the plague, hundreds of mankind exist and find a fair share of happiness in the world by the aid of the spinning jenny. And the great fire, at its worst, could not have burned the supply of coal, the daily working of which, in the bowels of the earth, made possible by the steam pump, gives rise to an amount of wealth to which the millions lost in old London are but as an old song . . .

However, there are blind leaders of the blind, and ...
According to them, the improvement of natural knowledge always has been, and always must be, synonymous with no more than the improvement of the material resources and the increase of the gratifications of men ... a sort of fairy godmother ready to furnish her pets with shoes of swiftness, swords of sharpness, and omnipotent Aladdin's lamps, so that they may have telegraphs to Saturn, and see the other side of the moon, and thank God they are better than their benighted ancestors.

If this talk were true, I, for one, should not greatly care to toil in the service of natural knowledge. I think I would just as soon be quietly chipping my own flint axe, after the manner of my forefathers a few thousand years back, as be troubled with the endless malady of thought which now infests us all, for such reward ...

I should not venture to speak thus strongly if my justification were not to be found in the simplest and most obvious facts, – if it needed more than an appeal to the most notorious truths to justify my assertion, that the improvement of natural knowledge, whatever direction it has taken, and however low the aims of those who may have commenced it – has not only conferred practical benefits on men, but, in so doing, has effected a revolution in their conceptions of the universe and of themselves, and has profoundly altered their modes of thinking and their views of right and wrong. I say that natural knowledge, seeking to satisfy natural wants, has found the ideas which can alone still spiritual cravings. I say that natural knowledge, in desiring to ascertain the laws of comfort, has been driven to discover those of conduct, and to lay the foundations of a new morality ...

Men have acquired the ideas of the practically infinite extent of the universe and of its practical eternity; they are familiar with the conception that our earth is but an infinitesimal fragment of that part of the universe which can be seen; and that, nevertheless, its duration is, as compared with our standards of time, infinite. They have further acquired the idea that man is but one of innumerable forms of life now existing on the globe, and that the present existences are but the last of an immeasurable series of predecessors. Moreover, every step they have made in natural knowledge has tended to extend and rivet in their minds the conception of a definite order of the universe ...

The improver of natural knowledge absolutely refuses to acknowledge authority, as such. For him, scepticism is the highest of duties; blind faith the one unpardonable sin. And it cannot be otherwise, for every great advance in natural knowledge has involved the absolute rejection of authority, the cherishing of the keenest scepticism, the annihilation of the spirit of blind faith ... The man of science has learned to believe in justification, not by faith, but by verification.

Thus, without for a moment pretending to despise the practical results of the improvement of natural knowledge, and its beneficial influence on material civilisation, it must, I think, be admitted that the great ideas, some of which I have indicated, and the ethical spirit which I have endeavoured to sketch ... constitute the real and permanent significance of natural knowledge.

If these ideas be destined, as I believe they are, to be more and more firmly established as the world grows older; if that spirit be fated, as I believe it is, to extend itself into all departments of human thought, and to become co-extensive with the range of knowledge ... then we, who are still children, may justly feel it our highest duty to recognise the advisableness of improving natural knowledge, and so to aid ourselves and our successors in our course towards the noble goal which lies before mankind.

Collected Essays, 1, 18–41
'Lay Sermon' in St Martin's Hall, Long Acre, 7 January 1866
Published in *The Fortnightly Review*, 3 (15 January 1866), 626
Reprinted in T. H. Huxley, *Lay Sermons, Addresses and Reviews* (Macmillan, 1870)

A LIBERAL EDUCATION;
AND WHERE TO FIND IT

(1868)

The business which the South London Working Men's College has undertaken is a great work; indeed, I might say, that Education, with which that college proposes to grapple, is the greatest work of all those which lie ready to a man's hand just at present.

And, at length, this fact is becoming generally recognised. You cannot go anywhere without hearing a buzz of more or less confused and contradictory talk on this subject – nor can you fail to notice that, in one point at any rate, there is a very decided advance upon like discussions in former days. Nobody outside the agricultural interest now dares to say that education is a bad thing. If any representative of the once large and powerful party, which, in former days, proclaimed this opinion, still exists in a semi-fossil state, he keeps his thoughts to himself. In fact, there is a chorus of voices, almost distressing in their harmony, raised in favour of the doctrine that education is the great panacea for human troubles, and that, if the country is not shortly to go to the dogs, everybody must be educated.

The politicians tell us, 'You must educate the masses because they are going to be masters.' The clergy join in the cry for education, for they affirm that the people are drifting away from church and chapel into the broadest infidelity. The manufacturers and the capitalists swell the chorus lustily. They declare that ignorance makes bad workmen; that England will soon be unable to turn out cotton goods, or steam engines, cheaper than other people; and then, Ichabod! Ichabod! the glory will be departed from us. And a few voices are lifted up in favour of the doctrine that the masses should be educated because they are men and women with unlimited capacities of being, doing, and suffering, and that it is as true now, as ever it was, that the people perish for lack of knowledge.

These members of the minority, with whom I confess I have a good deal of sympathy, are doubtful whether any of the other reasons urged in favour of the education of the people are of much value – whether, indeed, some of them are based upon either wise or noble grounds of action. They question if it be wise to tell people that you will do for them, out of fear of their power, what you have left undone, so long as your only motive was compassion for their weakness and their sorrows. And, if ignorance of everything which it is needful a ruler should know is likely to do so much harm in the governing classes of the future, why is it, they ask reasonably enough, that such ignorance in the governing classes of the past has not been viewed with equal horror ?

Compare the average artisan and the average country squire, and it may be doubted if you will find a pin to choose between the two in point of ignorance, class feeling, or prejudice. It is true that the ignorance is of a different sort – that the class feeling is in favour of a different class – and that the prejudice has a distinct savour of wrong-headedness in each case – but it is questionable if the one is either a bit better, or a bit worse, than the other. The old protectionist theory is the doctrine of trades unions as applied by the squires, and the modern trades unionism is the doctrine of the squires applied by the artisans. Why should we be worse off under one *régime* than under the other ?

Again, this sceptical minority asks the clergy to think whether it is really want of education which keeps the masses away from their ministrations – whether the most completely educated men are not as open to reproach on this score as the workmen; and whether, perchance, this may not indicate that it is not education which lies at the bottom of the matter?

Once more, these people, whom there is no pleasing, venture to doubt whether the glory, which rests upon being able to undersell all the rest of the world, is a very safe kind of glory – whether we may not purchase it too dear; especially if we allow education, which ought to be directed to the making of men, to be diverted into a process of manufacturing human tools, wonderfully adroit in the exercise of some technical industry, but good for nothing else.

And, finally, these people inquire whether it is the masses alone who need a reformed and improved education. They ask whether the richest of our public schools might not well be made to supply knowledge, as well as gentlemanly habits, a strong class feeling, and eminent proficiency in cricket. They seem to think that the noble foundations of our old universities are hardly fulfilling their functions in their present posture of half clerical seminaries, half racecourses, where men are trained to win a senior wrangleship, or a double-first, as horses are trained to win a cup, with as little reference to the needs of after-life in the case of the man as in that of the racer. And, while as zealous for education as the rest, they affirm that, if the education of the richer classes were such as to fit them to be the leaders and the governors of the poorer; and, if the education of the poorer classes were such as to enable them to appreciate really wise guidance and good governance, the politicians need not fear mob-law, nor the clergy lament their want of flocks, nor the capitalists prognosticate the annihilation of the prosperity of the country.

Such is the diversity of opinion upon the why and the wherefore of education. And my hearers will be prepared to expect that the practical recommendations which are put forward are not less discordant. There is a loud cry for compulsory education. We English, in spite of constant experience to the contrary, preserve a touching faith in the efficacy of acts of Parliament; and I believe we should have compulsory education in the course of next session, if there were the least probability that half a dozen leading statesmen of different parties would agree what that education should be.

Some hold that education without theology is worse than none. Others maintain, quite as strongly, that education with theology is in the same predicament. But this is certain, that those who hold the first opinion can by no means agree what theology should be taught; and that those who maintain the second are in a small minority.

At any rate 'make people learn to read, write, and cipher', say a great many; and the advice is undoubtedly sensible as far as it goes. But, as has happened to me in former days, those who, in despair of getting anything better, advocate this measure, are met with the objection that it is very like making a child practise the use of a knife, fork, and spoon, without giving it a particle of meat. I really don't know what reply is to be made to such an objection.

But it would be unprofitable to spend more time in disentangling, or rather in showing up the knots in, the ravelled skeins of our neighbours. Much more to the purpose is it to ask if we possess any clue of our own which may guide us among these entanglements. And by way of a beginning, let us ask ourselves – What is education? Above all things, what is our ideal of a thoroughly liberal education? – of that education which if we could begin life again we would give ourselves – of that education which, if we could mould the fates to our own will, we would give our children? Well, I know not what may be your conceptions upon this matter, but I will tell you mine, and I hope I shall find that our views are not very discrepant.

Suppose it were perfectly certain that the life and fortune of every one of us would, one day or other, depend upon his winning or losing a game at chess. Don't you think that we should all consider it to be a primary duty to learn at least the names of the moves of the pieces; to have a notion of a gambit, and a keen eye for all the means of giving and getting out of check? Do you not think that we should look with a disapprobation amounting to scorn, upon the father who allowed his son, or the state which allowed its members, to grow up without knowing a pawn from a knight?

Yet it is a very plain and elementary truth, that the life, the fortune, and the happiness of every one of us, and, more or less, of those who are connected with us, do depend upon our knowing something of the rules of a game infinitely more difficult and complicated than chess. It is a game which has been played for untold ages, every man and woman of us being one of the two players in a game of his or her own. The chess-board is the world, the pieces are the phenomena of the universe, the rules of the game are what we call the laws of Nature. The player on the other side is hidden from us. We know that his play is always fair, just and patient. But we also know, to our cost, that he never overlooks a mistake, or makes the smallest allowance for ignorance. To the man who plays well, the highest stakes are paid, with that sort of overflowing generosity with which the strong shows delight in strength. And one who plays ill is checkmated – without haste, but without remorse.

My metaphor will remind some of you of the famous picture in which Retzsch has depicted Satan playing at chess with man for his soul. Substitute for the mocking fiend in that picture a calm, strong angel who is playing for love, as we say, and would rather lose than win – and I should accept it as an image of human life.

Well, what I mean by Education is learning the rules of this mighty game. In other words, education is the instruction of the intellect in the laws of Nature, under which name I include not merely things and their forces, but men and their ways; and the fashioning of the affections and of the will into an earnest and loving desire to move in harmony with those laws. For me, education means neither more nor less than this. Anything which professes to call itself education must be tried by this standard, and if it fails to stand the test, I will not call it education, whatever may be the force of authority, or of numbers, upon the other side.

It is important to remember that, in strictness, there is no such thing as an uneducated man. Take an extreme case. Suppose that an adult man, in the full vigour of his faculties, could be suddenly placed in the world, as Adam is said to have been, and then left to do as he best might. How long would he be left uneducated? Not five minutes. Nature would begin to teach him, through the eye, the ear, the touch, the properties of objects. Pain and pleasure would be at his elbow telling him to do this and avoid that; and by slow degrees the man would receive an education which, if narrow, would be thorough, real, and adequate to his circumstances, though there would be no extras and very few accomplishments.

And if to this solitary man entered a second Adam, or, better still, an Eve, a new and greater world, that of social and moral phenomena, would be revealed. Joys and woes, compared with which all others might seem but faint shadows, would spring from the new relations. Happiness and sorrow would take the place of the coarser monitors, pleasure and pain; but conduct would still be shaped by the observation of the natural consequences of actions; or, in other words, by the laws of the nature of man.

To every one of us the world was once as fresh and new

as to Adam. And then, long before we were susceptible of any other mode of instruction, Nature took us in hand, and every minute of waking life brought its educational influence, shaping our actions into rough accordance with Nature's laws, so that we might not be ended untimely by too gross disobedience. Nor should I speak of this process of education as past for any one, be he as old as he may. For every man the world is as fresh as it was at the first day, and as full of untold novelties for him who has the eyes to see them. And Nature is still continuing her patient education of us in that great university, the universe, of which we are all members – Nature having no Test-Acts.

Those who take honours in Nature's university, who learn the laws which govern men and things and obey them, are the really great and successful men in this world. The great mass of mankind are the 'Poll', who pick up just enough to get through without much discredit. Those who won't learn at all are plucked; and then you can't come up again. Nature's pluck means extermination.

Thus the question of compulsory education is settled so far as Nature is concerned. Her bill on that question was framed and passed long ago. But, like all compulsory legislation, that of Nature is harsh and wasteful in its operation. Ignorance is visited as sharply as wilful disobedience – incapacity meets with the same punishment as crime. Nature's discipline is not even a word and a blow, and the blow first; but the blow without the word. It is left to you to find out why your ears are boxed.

The object of what we commonly call education – that education in which man intervenes and which I shall distinguish as artificial education – is to make good these defects in Nature's methods; to prepare the child to receive Nature's education, neither incapably nor ignorantly, nor with wilful disobedience; and to understand the preliminary symptoms of her pleasure, without waiting for the box on the ear. In short, all artificial education ought to be an anticipation of natural education. And a liberal education is an artificial education which has not only prepared a man to escape the great evils of disobedience to natural laws, but has trained him to appreciate and to seize upon the rewards, which Nature scatters with as free a hand as her penalties.

That man, I think, has had a liberal education who has been so trained in youth that his body is the ready servant of his will, and does with ease and pleasure all the work that, as a mechanism, it is capable of; whose intellect is a clear, cold, logic engine, with all its parts of equal strength, and in smooth working order; ready, like a steam engine, to be turned to any kind of work, and spin the gossamers as well as forge the anchors of the mind; whose mind is stored with a knowledge of the great and fundamental truths of Nature and of the laws of her operations; one who, no stunted ascetic, is full of life and fire, but whose passions are trained to come to heel by a vigorous will, the servant of a tender conscience; who has learned to love all beauty, whether of Nature or of art, to hate all vileness, and to respect others as himself.

Such an one and no other, I conceive, has had a liberal education; for he is, as completely as a man can be, in harmony with Nature. He will make the best of her, and she of him. They will get on together rarely: she as his ever beneficent mother; he as her mouthpiece, her conscious self, her minister and interpreter.

Where is such an education as this to be had ? Where is there any approximation to it ? Has any one tried to found such an education ? Looking over the length and breadth of these islands, I am afraid that all these questions must receive a negative answer. Consider our primary schools and what is taught in them. A child learns :–

1. To read, write, and cipher, more or less well; but

in a very large proportion of cases not so well as to take pleasure in reading, or to be able to write the commonest letter properly.

2. A quantity of dogmatic theology, of which the child, nine times out of ten, understands next to nothing.

3. Mixed up with this, so as to seem to stand or fall with it, a few of the broadest and simplest principles of morality. This, to my mind, is much as if a man of science should make the story of the fall of the apple in Newton's garden an integral part of the doctrine of gravitation, and teach it as of equal authority with the law of the inverse squares.

4. A good deal of Jewish history and Syrian geography, and perhaps a little something about English history and the geography of the child's own country. But I doubt if there is a primary school in England in which hangs a map of the hundred in which the village lies, so that the children may be practically taught by it what a map means.

5. A certain amount of regularity, attentive obedience, respect for others: obtained by fear, if the master be incompetent or foolish; by love and reverence, if he be wise.

So far as this school course embraces a training in the theory and practice of obedience to the moral laws of Nature, I gladly admit, not only that it contains a valuable educational element, but that, so far, it deals with the most valuable and important part of all education. Yet, contrast what is done in this direction with what might be done; with the time given to matters of comparatively no importance; with the absence of any attention to things of the highest moment; and one is tempted to think of Falstaff's bill and 'the halfpenny worth of bread to all that quantity of sack.'

Let us consider what a child thus 'educated' knows, and what it does not know. Begin with the most important topic of all – morality, as the guide of conduct. The child knows well enough that some acts meet with approbation and some with disapprobation. But it has never heard that there lies in the nature of things a reason for every moral law, as cogent and as well defined as that which underlies every physical law; that stealing and lying are just as certain to be followed by evil consequences, as putting your hand in the fire, or jumping out of a garret window. Again, though the scholar may have been made acquainted, in dogmatic fashion, with the broad laws of morality, he has no training in the application of those laws to the difficult problems which result from the complex conditions of modern civilisation. Would it not be very hard to expect any one to solve a problem in conic sections who had merely been taught the axioms and definitions of mathematical science?

A workman has to bear hard labour, and perhaps privation, while he sees others rolling in wealth, and feeding their dogs with what would keep his children from starvation. Would it not be well to have helped that man to calm the natural promptings of discontent by showing him, in his youth, the necessary connection of the moral law which prohibits stealing with the stability of society – by proving to him, once for all, that it is better for his own people, better for himself, better for future generations, that he should starve than steal? If you have no foundation of knowledge, or habit of thought, to work upon, what chance have you of persuading a hungry man that a capitalist is not a thief 'with a circumbendibus?' And if he honestly believes that, of what avail is it to quote the commandment against stealing, when he proposes to make the capitalist disgorge?

Again, the child learns absolutely nothing of the history or the political organisation of his own country. His general impression is, that everything of much importance happened a very long while ago; and that the Queen and the gentlefolks govern the country much after the fashion of King David and the elders and nobles of Israel – his sole models. Will you give a man with this much information a vote? In easy times he sells it for a pot of beer. Why should he not? It is of about as much use to him as a chignon, and he knows as much what to do with it, for any other purpose. In bad times, on the contrary, he applies his simple theory of government, and believes that his rulers are the cause of his sufferings – a belief which sometimes bears remarkable practical fruits.

Least of all, does the child gather from this primary 'education' of ours a conception of the laws of the physical world, or of the relations of cause and effect therein. And this is the more to be lamented, as the poor are especially exposed to physical evils, and are more interested in removing them than any other class of the community. If any one is concerned in knowing the ordinary laws of mechanics one would think it is the hand-labourer, whose daily toil lies among levers and pulleys; or among the other implements of artisan work. And if any one is interested in the laws of health, it is the poor workman, whose strength is wasted by ill-prepared food, whose health is sapped by bad ventilation and bad drainage, and half whose children are massacred by disorders which might be prevented. Not only does our present primary education carefully abstain from hinting to the workman that some of his greatest evils are traceable to mere physical agencies, which could be removed by energy, patience, and frugality; but it does worse – it renders him, so far as it can, deaf to those who could help him, and tries to substitute an Oriental submission to what is falsely declared to be the will of God, for his natural tendency to strive after a better condition.

What wonder, then, if very recently an appeal has been made to statistics for the profoundly foolish purpose of showing that education is of no good – that it diminishes neither misery nor crime among the masses of mankind? I reply, why should the thing which has been called education do either the one or the other? If I am a knave or a fool, teaching me to read and write won't make me less of either one or the other – unless somebody shows me how to put my reading and writing to wise and good purposes.

Suppose any one were to argue that medicine is of no use, because it could be proved statistically, that the percentage of deaths was just the same among people who had been taught how to open a medicine chest, and among those who did not so much as know the key by sight. The argument is absurd; but it is not more preposterous than that against which I am contending. The only medicine for suffering, crime, and all the other woes of mankind, is wisdom. Teach a man to read and write, and you have put into his hands the great keys of the wisdom box. But it is quite another matter whether he ever opens the box or not. And he is as likely to poison as to cure himself, if, without guidance, he swallows the first drug that comes to hand. In these times a man may as well be purblind, as unable to read – lame, as unable to write. But I protest that, if I thought the alternative were a necessary one, I would rather that the children of the poor should grow up ignorant of both these mighty arts, than that they should remain ignorant of that knowledge to which these arts are means.

It may be said that all these animadversions may apply to primary schools, but that the higher schools, at any rate, must be allowed to give a liberal education. In fact they professedly sacrifice everything else to this object.

Let us inquire into this matter. What do the higher schools, those to which the great middle class of the country sends its children, teach, over and above the instruction given in the primary schools? There is a little

7

more reading and writing of English. But, for all that, every one knows that it is a rare thing to find a boy of the middle or upper classes who can read aloud decently, or who can put his thoughts on paper in clear and grammatical (to say nothing of good or elegant) language. The 'ciphering' of the lower schools expands into elementary mathematics in the higher; into arithmetic, with a little algebra, a little Euclid. But I doubt if one boy in five hundred has ever heard the explanation of a rule of arithmetic, or knows his Euclid otherwise than by rote.

Of theology, the middle class schoolboy gets rather less than poorer children, less absolutely and less relatively, because there are so many other claims upon his attention. I venture to say that, in the great majority of cases, his ideas on this subject when he leaves school are of the most shadowy and vague description, and associated with painful impressions of the weary hours spent in learning collects and catechism by heart.

Modern geography, modern history, modern literature; the English language as a language; the whole circle of the sciences, physical, moral and social, are even more completely ignored in the higher than in the lower schools. Up till within a few years back, a boy might have passed through any one of the great public schools with the greatest distinction and credit, and might never so much as have heard of one of the subjects I have just mentioned. He might never have heard that the earth goes round the sun; that England underwent a great revolution in 1688, and France another in 1789; that there once lived certain notable men called Chaucer, Shakespeare, Milton, Voltaire, Goethe, Schiller. The first might be a German and the last an Englishman for anything he could tell you to the contrary. And as for Science, the only idea the word would suggest to his mind would be dexterity in boxing.

I have said that this was the state of things a few years

back, for the sake of the few righteous who are to be found among the educational cities of the plain. But I would not have you too sanguine about the result, if you sound the minds of the existing generation of public schoolboys, on such topics as those I have mentioned.

Now let us pause to consider this wonderful state of affairs; for the time will come when Englishmen will quote it as the stock example of the stolid stupidity of their ancestors in the nineteenth century. The most thoroughly commercial people, the greatest voluntary wanderers and colonists the world has ever seen, are precisely the middle classes of this country. If there be a people which has been busy making history on the great scale for the last three hundred years – and the most profoundly interesting history – history which, if it happened to be that of Greece or Rome, we should study with avidity – it is the English. If there be a people which, during the same period, has developed a remarkable literature, it is our own. If there be a nation whose prosperity depends absolutely and wholly upon their mastery over the forces of Nature, upon their intelligent apprehension of, and obedience to the laws of the creation and distribution of wealth, and of the stable equilibrium of the forces of society, it is precisely this nation. And yet this is what these wonderful people tell their sons: – 'At the cost of from one to two thousand pounds of our hard-earned money, we devote twelve of the most precious years of your lives to school. There you shall toil, or be supposed to toil; but there you shall not learn one single thing of all those you will most want to know directly you leave school and enter upon the practical business of life. You will in all probability go into business, but you shall not know where, or how, any article of commerce is produced, or the difference between an export or an import, or the meaning of the word "capital". You will very likely settle in a colony, but you shall not know whether Tasmania is part of New South Wales, or *vice versa*.

'Very probably you may become a manufacturer, but you shall not be provided with the means of understanding the working of one of your own steam-engines, or the nature of the raw products you employ; and, when you are asked to buy a patent, you shall not have the slightest means of judging whether the inventor is an imposter who is contravening the elementary principles of science, or a man who will make you as rich as Croesus.

'You will very likely get into the House of Commons. You will have to take your share in making laws which may prove a blessing or a curse to millions of men. But you shall not hear one word respecting the political organisation of your country; the meaning of the controversy between free-traders and protectionists shall never have been mentioned to you; you shall not so much as know that there are such things as economical laws.

'The mental power which will be of most importance in your daily life will be the power of seeing things as they are without regard to authority; and of drawing accurate general conclusions from particular facts. But at school and at college you shall know of no source of truth but authority; nor exercise your reasoning faculty upon anything but deduction from that which is laid down by authority.

'You will have to weary your soul with work, and many a time eat your bread in sorrow and in bitterness, and you shall not have learned to take refuge in the great source of pleasure without alloy, the serene resting-place for worn human nature, – the world of art.'

Said I not rightly that we are a wonderful people? I am quite prepared to allow, that education entirely devoted to these omitted subjects might not be a completely liberal education. But is an education which ignores them all a liberal education? Nay, is it too much to say that the education which should embrace these subjects and no others would be a real education, though an incomplete one; while an education which omits them is really not an education at all, but a more or less useful course of intellectual gymnastics?

For what does the middle-class school put in the place of all these things which are left out? It substitutes what is usually comprised under the compendious title of the 'classics' – that is to say, the languages, the literature, and the history of the ancient Greeks and Romans, and the geography of so much of the world as was known to these two great nations of antiquity. Now, do not expect me to depreciate the earnest and enlightened pursuit of classical learning. I have not the least desire to speak ill of such occupations, nor any sympathy with those who run them down. On the contrary, if my opportunities had lain in that direction, there is no investigation into which I could have thrown myself with greater delight than that of antiquity.

What science can present greater attractions than philology? How can a lover of literary excellence fail to rejoice in the ancient masterpieces? And with what consistency could I, whose business lies so much in the attempt to decipher the past, and to build up intelligible forms out of the scattered fragments of long-extinct beings, fail to take a sympathetic, though an unlearned, interest in the labours of a Niebuhr, a Gibbon, or a Grote? Classical history is a great section of the palaeontology of man; and I have the same double respect for it as for other kinds of palaeontology – that is to say, a respect for the facts which it establishes as for all facts, and a still greater respect for it as a preparation for the discovery of a law of progress.

But if the classics were taught as they might be taught – if boys and girls were instructed in Greek and Latin, not merely as languages, but as illustrations of philological science; if a vivid picture of life on the shores of the Mediterranean two thousand years ago were imprinted on the minds of scholars; if ancient history were taught, not as a weary series of feuds and fights, but traced to its causes in such men placed under such conditions; if, lastly, the study of the classical books were followed in such a manner as to impress boys with their beauties, and with the grand simplicity of their statement of the ever-lasting problems of human life, instead of with their verbal and grammatical peculiarities; I still think it as little proper that they should form the basis of a liberal education for our contemporaries, as I should think it fitting to make that sort of palaeontology with which I am familiar the back-bone of modern education.

It is wonderful how close a parallel to classical training could be made out of that palaeontology to which I refer. In the first place I could get up an osteological primer so arid, so pedantic in its terminology, so altogether distasteful to the youthful mind, as to beat the recent famous produc-tion of the head-masters out of the field in all these excel-lences. Next, I could exercise my boys upon easy fossils, and bring out all their powers of memory and all their ingenuity in the application of my osteo-grammatical rules to the interpretation, or construing, of those fragments. To those who had reached the higher classes, I might supply odd bones to be built up into animals, giving great honour and reward to him who succeeded in fabricating monsters most entirely in accordance with the rules. That would answer to verse-making and essay-writing in the dead languages.

To be sure, if a great comparative anatomist were to look at these fabrications he might shake his head, or laugh. But what then? Would such a catastrophe destroy the parallel? What, think you, would Cicero, or Horace, say to the production of the best sixth form going? And would not Terence stop his ears and run out if he could be present at an English performance of his own plays? Would *Hamlet*, in the mouths of a set of French actors, who should insist on pronouncing English after the fashion of their own tongue, be more hideously ridiculous?

But it will be said that I am forgetting the beauty, and the human interest, which appertain to classical studies. To this I reply that it is only a very strong man who can appreciate the charms of a landscape as he is toiling up a steep hill, along a bad road. What with short-windedness, stones, ruts, and a pervading sense of the wisdom of rest and be thankful, most of us have little enough sense of the beautiful under these circumstances. The ordinary school-boy is precisely in this case. He finds Parnassus uncommonly steep, and there is no chance of his having much time or inclination to look about him till he gets to the top. And nine times out of ten he does not get to the top.

But if this be a fair picture of the results of classical teaching at its best – and I gather from those who have authority to speak on such matters that it is so – what is to be said of classical teaching at its worst, or in other words, of the classics of our ordinary middle-class schools? I will tell you. It means getting up endless forms and rules by heart. It means turning Latin and Greek into English, for the mere sake of being able to do it, and without the smallest regard to the worth, or worthlessness, of the author read. It means the learning of innumerable, not always decent, fables in such a shape that the meaning they once had is dried up into utter trash; and the only impression left upon a boy's mind is, that the people who believed such things must have been the greatest idiots the world ever saw. And it means, finally, that after a dozen years spent at this kind of work, the sufferer shall be incompetent to interpret a passage in an author he had not already got up; that he shall loathe the sight of a Greek or Latin book; and that he shall never open, or think of, a classical writer again, until, wonderful to relate, he insists upon submitting his sons to the same process.

These be your gods, O Israel! For the sake of this net result (and respectability) the British father denies his children all the knowledge they might turn to account in life, not merely for the achievement of vulgar success, but for guidance in the great crises of human existence. This is the stone he offers to those whom he is bound by the strongest and tenderest ties to feed with bread.

If primary and secondary education are in this unsatisfactory state, what is to be said to the universities? This is an awful subject, and one I almost fear to touch with my unhallowed hands; but I can tell you what those say who have authority to speak.

The Rector of Lincoln College, in his lately published valuable 'Suggestions for Academical Organisation with especial reference to Oxford', tells us (p. 127):–

The colleges were, in their origin, endowments, not for the elements of a general liberal education, but for the prolonged study of special and professional faculties by men of riper age. The universities embraced both these objects. The colleges, while they incidentally aided in elementary education, were specially devoted to the highest learning . . .

This was the theory of the middle-age university and the design of collegiate foundations in their origin. Time and circumstances have brought about a total change. The colleges no longer promote the researches of science, or direct professional study. Here and there college walls may shelter an occasional student, but not in larger proportions than may be found in private life. Elementary teaching of youths under twenty is now the only function performed by the university, and almost the only object of college endowments. Colleges were homes for the life-study of the highest and most abstruse parts of knowledge. They have become boarding schools in which the elements of the learned languages are taught to youths.

If Mr. Pattison's high position, and his obvious love and
respect for his university, be insufficient to convince the
outside world that language so severe is yet no more than
just, the authority of the Commissioners who reported on
the University of Oxford in 1850 is open to no challenge.
Yet they write:–

It is generally acknowledged that both Oxford and the country at
large suffer greatly from the absence of a body of learned men
devoting their lives to the cultivation of science, and to the direction of academical education.

The fact that so few books of profound research emanate
from the University of Oxford, materially impairs its character
as a seat of learning, and consequently its hold on the respect of
the nation.

Cambridge can claim no exemption from the reproaches
addressed to Oxford. And thus there seems no escape
from the admission that what we fondly call our great
seats of learning are simply 'boarding schools' for bigger
boys; that learned men are not more numerous in them
than out of them; that the advancement of knowledge is
not the object of fellows of colleges; that, in the philosophic
calm and meditative stillness of their greenswarded courts,
philosophy does not thrive, and meditation bears few
fruits.

It is my great good fortune to reckon amongst my
friends resident members of both universities, who are
men of learning and research, zealous cultivators of science,
keeping before their minds a noble ideal of a university,
and doing their best to make that ideal a reality; and, to me,
they would necessarily typify the universities, did not the
authoritative statements I have quoted compel me to
believe that they are exceptional, and not representative
men. Indeed, upon calm consideration, several circumstances lead me to think that the Rector of Lincoln College
and the Commissioners cannot be far wrong.

I believe there can be no doubt that the foreigner who should wish to become acquainted with the scientific, or the literary, activity of modern England, would simply lose his time and his pains if he visited our universities with that object.

And, as for works of profound research on any subject, and, above all, in that classical lore for which the universities profess to sacrifice almost everything else, why, a third-rate, poverty-stricken German university turns out more produce of that kind in one year, than our vast and wealthy foundations elaborate in ten.

Ask the man who is investigating any question, profoundly and thoroughly – be it historical, philosophical, philological, physical, literary, or theological; who is trying to make himself master of any abstract subject (except, perhaps, political economy and geology, both of which are intensely Anglican sciences), whether he is not compelled to read half a dozen times as many German as English books? And whether, of these English books, more than one in ten is the work of a fellow of a college, or a professor of an English university?

Is this from any lack of power in the English as compared with the German mind? The countrymen of Grote and of Mill, of Faraday, of Robert Brown, of Lyell, and of Darwin, to go no further back than the contemporaries of men of middle age, can afford to smile at such a suggestion. England can show now, as she has been able to show in every generation since civilisation spread over the West, individual men who hold their own against the world, and keep alive the old tradition of her intellectual eminence.

But, in the majority of cases, these men are what they are in virtue of their native intellectual force, and of a strength of character which will not recognise impediments. They are not trained in the courts of the Temple of

Science, but storm the walls of that edifice in all sorts of irregular ways, and with much loss of time and power, in order to obtain their legitimate positions.

Our universities not only do not encourage such men; do not offer them positions, in which it should be their highest duty to do, thoroughly, that which they are most capable of doing; but, as far as possible, university training shuts out of the minds of those among them, who are subjected to it, the prospect that there is anything in the world for which they are specially fitted. Imagine the success of the attempt to still the intellectual hunger of any of the men I have mentioned, by putting before him as the object of existence, the successful mimicry of the measure of a Greek song, or the roll of Ciceronian prose! Imagine how much success would be likely to attend the attempt to persuade such men that the education which leads to perfection in such elegances is alone to be called culture; while the facts of history, the process of thought, the conditions of moral and social existence, and the laws of physical nature are left to be dealt with as they may by outside barbarians!

It is not thus that the German universities, from being beneath notice a century ago, have become what they are now – the most intensely cultivated and the most productive intellectual corporations the world has ever seen.

The student who repairs to them sees in the list of classes and of professors a fair picture of the world of knowledge. Whatever he needs to know there is some one ready to teach him, some one competent to discipline him in the way of learning; whatever his special bent, let him but be able and diligent, and in due time he shall find distinction and a career. Among his professors, he sees men whose names are known and revered throughout the civilised world; and their living example infects him with a noble ambition, and a love for the spirit of work.

The Germans dominate the intellectual world by virtue of the same simple secret as that which made Napoleon the master of old Europe. They have declared *la carrière ouverte aux talents*, and every Bursch marches with a professor's gown in his knapsack. Let him become a great scholar, or a man of science, and ministers will compete for his services. In Germany, they do not leave the chance of his holding the office he would render illustrious to the tender mercies of a hot canvass, and the final wisdom of a mob of country parsons.

In short, in Germany, the universities are exactly what the Rector of Lincoln and the Commissioners tell us the English universities are not; that is to say, corporations 'of learned men devoting their lives to the cultivation of science, and the direction of academical education.' They are not 'boarding schools for youths,' nor clerical seminaries; but institutions for the higher culture of men, in which the theological faculty is of no more importance, or prominence, than the rest; and which are truly 'universities', since they strive to represent and embody the totality of human knowledge, and to find room for all forms of intellectual activity.

May zealous and clear-headed reformers like Mr. Pattison succeed in their noble endeavours to shape our universities towards some such ideal as this, without losing what is valuable and distinctive in their social tone! But until they have succeeded, a liberal education will be no more obtainable in our Oxford and Cambridge Universities than in our public schools.

If I am justified in my conception of the ideal of a liberal education; and if what I have said about the existing educational institutions of the country is also true, it is clear that the two have no sort of relation to one another; that the best of our schools and the most complete of our university trainings give but a narrow, one-sided, and essentially illiberal education – while the worst give what is really next to no education at all. The South London Working-Men's College could not copy any of these institutions if it would; I am bold enough to express the conviction that it ought not if it could.

For what is wanted is the reality and not the mere name of a liberal education; and this College must steadily set before itself the ambition to be able to give that education sooner or later. At present we are but beginning, sharpening our educational tools, as it were, and, except a modicum of physical science, we are not able to offer much more than is to be found in an ordinary school.

Moral and social science – one of the greatest and most fruitful of our future classes, I hope – at present lacks only one thing in our programme, and that is a teacher. A considerable want, no doubt; but it must be recollected that it is much better to want a teacher than to want the desire to learn.

Further, we need what, for want of a better name, I must call Physical Geography. What I mean is that which the Germans call '*Erdkunde*'. It is a description of the earth, of its place and relation to other bodies; of its general structure, and of its great features – winds, tides, mountains, plains: of the chief forms of the vegetable and animal worlds, of the varieties of man. It is the peg upon which the greatest quantity of useful and entertaining scientific information can be suspended.

Literature is not upon the College programme; but I hope some day to see it there. For literature is the greatest of all sources of refined pleasure, and one of the great uses of a liberal education is to enable us to enjoy that pleasure. There is scope enough for the purposes of liberal education in the study of the rich treasures of our own language alone. All that is needed is direction, and the cultivation of a refined taste by attention to sound criticism. But there is no reason why French and German should not be mastered sufficiently to read what is worth reading in those languages with pleasure and with profit.

And finally, by and by, we must have History; treated not as a succession of battles and dynasties; not as a series of biographies; not as evidence that Providence has always been on the side of either Whigs or Tories; but as the development of man in times past, and in other conditions than our own.

But, as it is one of the principles of our College to be self-supporting, the public must lead, and we must follow, in these matters. If my hearers take to heart what I have said about liberal education, they will desire these things, and I doubt not we shall be able to supply them. But we must wait till the demand is made.

Collected Essays, III, 76–110

Address at the opening of the South London Working Men's College, Southwark, 4 January 1868

Summary published in *South London Press* (11 January 1868)

Fuller version in *The Quarterly Journal of Education*, 1 (February 1868), 145, under the title, 'Professor Huxley's Inaugural Address on Education at the Opening of the South London Working Men's College'

Full text in *Macmillan's Magazine*, XVII (March 1868), 367

Reprinted in T. H. Huxley, *Lay Sermons, Addresses and Reviews* (Macmillan, 1870)

SCIENTIFIC EDUCATION:
NOTES OF AN AFTER-DINNER SPEECH

(1869)

The introduction of scientific training into the general education of the country is a topic upon which I could not have spoken, without some more or less apologetic introduction, a few years ago. But upon this, as upon other matters, public opinion has of late undergone a rapid modification. Committees of both Houses of the Legislature have agreed that something must be done in this direction, and have even thrown out timid and faltering suggestions as to what should be done; while at the opposite pole of society, committees of working men have expressed their conviction that scientific training is the one thing needful for their advancement, whether as men, or as workmen . . .

The heads of colleges in our great universities (who have not the reputation of being the most mobile of persons) have, in several cases, thought it well that, out of the great number of honours and rewards at their disposal, a few should hereafter be given to the cultivators of the physical [natural] sciences . . . and physical science, even now, constitutes a recognised element of the school curriculum in Harrow and Rugby . . .

At other times, and in other places, I have endeavoured to state the higher and more abstract arguments, by which the study of physical science may be shown to be indispensable to the complete training of the human mind; but I do not wish it to be supposed that . . . I am insensible to the weight which ought to be attached to that which has been said to be the English conception of Paradise –

namely, 'getting on' . . . humanity is so constituted that a vast number of us would never be impelled to those stretches of exertion which make us wiser and more capable men, if it were not for . . . the purpose of 'getting on' in the most practical sense.

Now the value of a knowledge of physical science as a means of getting on is indubitable. There are hardly any of our trades, except the merely huckstering ones, in which some knowledge of science may not be directly profitable to the pursuer of that occupation. As industry attains higher stages of its development, as its processes become more complicated and refined, and competition more keen, the sciences are dragged in, one by one, to take their share in the fray; and he who can best avail himself of their help is the man who will come out uppermost in that struggle for existence, which goes on as fiercely beneath the smooth surface of modern society, as among the wild inhabitants of the woods.

But in addition to the bearing of science on ordinary practical life, let me direct your attention to its immense influence on several of the professions . . . I appeal to those who know what engineering is, to say how far I am right in respect to that profession; but with regard to another, of no less importance, I shall venture to speak of my own knowledge. There is no one of us who may not at any moment be thrown, bound hand and foot by physical incapacity, into the hands of the medical practitioner. The chances of life and death for all and each of us may, at any moment, depend on the skill with which that practitioner is able to make out what is wrong in our bodily frames, and on his ability to apply the proper remedy to the defect . . .

There is another profession, to the members of which I think, a certain preliminary knowledge of physical science might be quite as valuable as to the medical man . . . Like the medical profession, the clerical, of which I now speak, rests its power to heal upon its knowledge of the order of the universe – upon certain theories of man's relation to that which lies outside him. It is not my business to express any opinion about these theories. I merely wish to point out that, like all other theories, they are professedly based upon matters of fact ... Why do not the clergy as a body acquire, as a part of their preliminary education, some such tincture of physical science as will put them in a position to understand the difficulties in the way of accepting their theories, which are forced upon the mind of every thoughtful and intelligent man, who has taken the trouble to instruct himself in the elements of natural knowledge? ...

I think it would be better, not only for them, but for us. The army of liberal thought is, at present, in very loose order; and many a spirited free-thinker makes use of his freedom mainly to vent nonsense. We should be the better for a vigorous and watchful enemy to hammer us into cohesion and discipline; and I, for one, lament that the bench of Bishops cannot show a man of the calibre of Butler of the 'Analogy' ...

The next question to which I have to address myself is, What sciences ought to be thus taught? And this is one of the most important of questions, because my side (I am afraid I am a terribly candid friend) sometimes spoils its cause by going in for too much. There are other forms of culture beside physical science; and I should be profoundly sorry to see the fact forgotten, or even to observe a tendency to starve, or cripple, literary, or aesthetic, culture for the sake of science. Such a narrow view of the nature of education has nothing to do with my firm conviction that a complete and thorough scientific culture ought to be introduced into all schools. By this, however, I do not mean that every schoolboy should be taught everything in science. That would be a very absurd thing to conceive, and a very mischievous thing to attempt. What I mean is, that no boy or girl should leave school without possessing a grasp of the general character of science, and without having been disciplined, more or less, in the methods of all sciences; so that, when turned into the world to make their own way, they shall be prepared to face scientific problems . . . by being familiar with the general current of scientific thought, and by being able to apply the methods of science in the proper way. . .

To begin with, let every child be instructed in those general views of the phaenomena of Nature for which we have no exact English name . . . a general knowledge of the earth, and what is on it, and about it. . . . The child asks, 'What is the moon, and why does it shine?' 'What is this water, and where does it run?' 'What is the wind?' 'What makes the waves in the sea?' 'Where does this animal live, and what is the use of that plant?' And if not snubbed and stunted by being told not to ask foolish questions, there is no limit to the intellectual craving of a young child; nor any bounds to the slow, but solid, accretion of knowledge and development of the thinking faculty in this way. To all such questions, answers which are necessarily incomplete, though true as far as they go, may be given by any teacher whose ideas represent real knowledge and not mere book learning; and a panoramic view of Nature, accompanied by a strong infusion of the scientific habit of mind, may thus be placed within the reach of every child of nine or ten.

After this preliminary opening of the eyes to the great spectacle of the daily progress of Nature, as the reasoning faculties of the child grow, and he becomes familiar with the use of the tools of knowledge – reading, writing, and elementary mathematics – he should pass on to what is, in the more strict sense, physical science. Now there are two kinds of physical science: the one regards form and the relation of forms to one another; the other deals with causes and effects. In many of what we term sciences, these two kinds are mixed up together; but systematic botany is a pure example of the former kind, and physics of the latter kind, of science. ... Indeed, I conceive it would be one of the greatest boons which could be conferred upon England, if henceforward every child in the country were instructed in the general knowledge of the things about it, in the elements of physics, and of botany. But I should be still better pleased if there could be added somewhat of chemistry, and an elementary acquaintance with human physiology . . .

If the great benefits of scientific training are sought, it is essential that such training should be real: that is to say, that the mind of the scholar should be brought into direct relation with fact, that he should not merely be told a thing, but made to see . . . that the thing is so and no otherwise. The great peculiarity of scientific training, that in virtue of which it cannot be replaced by any other discipline whatsoever, is this bringing of the mind directly into contact with fact, and practising the intellect in the completest form of induction; that is to say, in drawing conclusions from particular facts made known by immediate observation of Nature . . .

That is to say, in explaining to a child the general phaenomena of Nature, you must, as far as possible, give reality to your teaching by object-lessons; in teaching him botany, he must handle the plants and dissect the flowers for himself; in teaching him physics . . . Don't be satisfied with telling him that a magnet attracts iron. Let him see that it does; let him feel the pull of the one upon the other for himself. And, especially, tell him that it is his duty to doubt until he is compelled, by the absolute authority of

Nature, to believe that which is written in books. Pursue this discipline carefully and conscientiously, and you may make sure that, however scanty may be the measure of information which you have poured into the boy's mind, you have created an intellectual habit of priceless value in practical life.

One is constantly asked, When should this scientific education be commenced? I should say with the dawn of intelligence...

People talk of the difficulty of teaching young children such matters, and in the same breath insist upon their learning their Catechism, which contains propositions far harder to comprehend than anything in the educational course I have proposed. Again: I am incessantly told that we, who advocate the introduction of science in schools, make no allowance for the stupidity of the average boy or girl; but, in my belief, that stupidity, in nine cases out of ten, *'fit, non nascitur'*, and is developed by a long process of parental and pedagogic repression of the natural intellectual appetites, accompanied by a persistent attempt to create artificial ones for food which is not only tasteless, but essentially indigestible.

Those who urge the difficulty of instructing young people in science are apt to forget another very important condition of success – important in all kinds of teaching, but most essential, I am disposed to think, when the scholars are very young. This condition is, that the teacher should himself really and practically know his subject. If he does, he will be able to speak of it in the easy language, and with the completeness of conviction, with which he talks of any ordinary every-day matter. If he does not, he will be afraid to wander beyond the limits of the technical phraseology which he has got up; and a dead dogmatism, which oppresses, or raises opposition, will take the place of the lively confidence, born of personal conviction, which cheers and encourages the eminently sympathetic mind of childhood.

I have already hinted that such scientific training as we seek for may be given without making any extravagant claim upon the time now devoted to education. We ask only for 'a most favoured nation' clause in our treaty with the schoolmaster; we demand no more than that science shall have as much time given to it as any other single subject – say four hours a week in each class of an ordinary school.

For the present, I think men of science would be well content with such an arrangement as this; but speaking for myself, I do not pretend to believe that such an arrangement can be, or will be, permanent. In these times the educational tree seems to me to have its roots in the air, its leaves and flowers in the ground; and, I confess, I should very much like to turn it upside down, so that its roots might be solidly embedded among the facts of Nature, and draw thence a sound nutriment for the foliage and fruit of literature and of art. No educational system can have a claim to permanence, unless it recognises the truth that education has two great ends to which everything else must be subordinated. The one of these is to increase knowledge; the other is to develop the love of right and the hatred of wrong ... there is perhaps no sight in the whole world more saddening and revolting than is offered by men sunk in ignorance of everything but what other men have written; seemingly devoid of moral belief or guidance; but with the sense of beauty so keen, and the power of expression so cultivated, that their sensual caterwauling may be almost mistaken for the music of the spheres ... I think I do not err in saying that if science were made a foundation of education, instead of being, at most, stuck on as cornice to the edifice, this state of things could not exist.

In advocating the introduction of physical science as a leading element in education, I by no means refer only to the higher schools. On the contrary, I believe that such a change is even more imperatively called for in those primary schools, in which the children of the poor are expected to turn to the best account the little time they can devote to the acquisition of knowledge. A great step in this direction has already been made by the establishment of science-classes under the Department of Science and Art, – a measure which came into existence unnoticed, but which will, I believe, turn out to be of more importance to the welfare of the people than many political changes over which the noise of battle has rent the air . . .

And this leads me to ask, Why should scientific teaching be limited to week-days ? Ecclesiastically-minded persons are in the habit of calling things they do not like by very hard names, and I should not wonder if they brand the proposition I am about to make as blasphemous, and worse. But, not minding this, I venture to ask, Would there really be anything wrong in using part of Sunday for the purpose of instructing those who have no other leisure, in a know-ledge of the phaenomena of Nature, and of man's relation to Nature ?

I should like to see a scientific Sunday-school in every parish, not for the purpose of superseding any existing means of teaching the people the things that are for their good, but side by side with them. . . . And if any of the ecclesiastical persons to whom I have referred, object that they find it derogatory to the honour of the God whom they worship, to awaken the minds of the young to the infinite wonder and majesty of the works which they proclaim His, and to teach them those laws which must needs be His laws, and therefore of all things needful for man to know – I can only recommend them to be let blood and put on a low diet . . .

Collected Essays, III, 111–33

Address to Liverpool Philomathic Society, Royal Hotel, Liverpool, 7 April 1869

Published in *Macmillan's Magazine*, xx (June 1869), 177

Reprinted in T. H. Huxley, *Lay Sermons, Addresses and Reviews* (Macmillan, 1870)

THE SCHOOL BOARDS:
WHAT THEY CAN DO,
AND WHAT THEY MAY DO

(1870)

An electioneering manifesto would be out of place in the pages of this Review; but any suspicion that may arise in the mind of the reader that the following pages partake of that nature, will be dispelled, if he reflect that they cannot be published until after the day on which the rate-payers of the metropolis will have decided which candidates for seats upon the Metropolitan School Board they will take, and which they will leave.

As one of those candidates, I may be permitted to say, that I feel much in the frame of mind of the Irish brick-layer's labourer, who bet another that he could not carry him to the top of the ladder in his hod. The challenged hodsman won his wager, but as the stakes were handed over, the challenger wistfully remarked, 'I'd great hopes of falling at the third round from the top'. .... But whether fortune befriend me in this rough method, or not, I should like to submit to those of whom I am potential, but of whom I may not be an actual colleague, and to others who may be interested in this most important problem – how to get the Education Act to work efficiently – some considerations as to what are the duties of the members of the School Boards, and what are the limits of their power.

I suppose no one will be disposed to dispute the proposition, that the prime duty of every member of such a Board is to endeavour to administer the Act honestly; or in accordance, not only with its letter, but with its spirit.

And if so, it would seem that the first step towards this very desirable end is, to obtain a clear notion of what that letter signifies, and what that spirit implies; or, in other words, what the clauses of the Act are intended to enjoin and to forbid . . .

Let us consider how this will work in practice. A school established by a School Board may receive support from three sources – from the rates, the school fees, and the Parliamentary grant. The latter may be as great as the two former taken together; and as it may be assumed, without much risk of error, that a constant pressure will be exerted by the ratepayers on the members who represent them to get as much out of the Government, and as little out of the rates, as possible, the School Boards will have a very strong motive for shaping the education they give, as nearly as may be, on the model which the Education Minister offers for their imitation, and for the copying of which he is prepared to pay . . .

I cannot but think, then, that the School Boards will have the appearance, but not the reality, of freedom of action, in regard to the subject-matter of what is commonly called 'secular' education.

As respects what is commonly called 'religious' education, the power of the Minister of Education is even more despotic. An interest, almost amounting to pathos, attaches itself, in my mind, to the frantic exertions which are at present going on in almost every school division, to elect certain candidates whose names have never before been heard of in connection with education, and who are either sectarian partisans, or nothing. In my own particular division, a body organised *ad hoc* is moving heaven and earth to get the seven seats filled by seven gentlemen, four of whom are good Churchmen, and three no less good Dissenters. But why should this seven times heated fiery furnace of theological zeal be so desirous to shed its genial warmth over the London School Board? Can it be that these zealous sectaries mean to evade the solemn pledge given in the Act?

'*No religious catechism or religious formulary which is distinctive of any particular denomination shall be taught in the school*' . . .

Supposing that the London School Board contains, as it probably will do, a majority of sectaries; and that they carry over the heads of a minority, a resolution that certain theological formulas, about which they all happen to agree, – say, for example, the doctrine of the Trinity, – shall be taught in the schools. Do they fondly imagine that the minority will not at once dispute their interpretation of the Act, and appeal to the Education Department to settle that dispute? And if so, do they suppose that any Minister of Education, who wants to keep his place, will tighten boundaries which the Legislature has left loose; and will give 'a final decision' which shall be offensive to every Unitarian and to every Jew in the House of Commons, besides creating a precedent which will afterwards be used to the injury of every Nonconformist? . . .

So much for the powers of the School Boards. Limited as they seem to be, it by no means follows that such Boards, if they are composed of intelligent and practical men, really more in earnest about education than about sectarian squabbles, may not exert a very great amount of influence. And, from many circumstances, this is especially likely to be the case with the London School Board, which, if it conducts itself wisely, may become a true educational parliament, as subordinate in authority to the Minister of Education, theoretically, as the Legislature is to the Crown, and yet, like the Legislature, possessed of great practical authority. And I suppose that no Minister of Education would be other than glad to have the aid of the deliberations of such a body, or fail to pay careful attention to its recommendations.

What, then, ought to be the nature and scope of the education which a School Board should endeavour to give to every child under its influence, and for which it should try to obtain the aid of the Parliamentary grants? In my judgment it should include at least the following kinds of instruction and of discipline:—

1. Physical training and drill, as part of the regular business of the school.

It is impossible to insist too much on the importance of this part of education for the children of the poor of great towns. All the conditions of their lives are unfavourable to their physical well-being. They are badly lodged, badly housed, badly fed, and live from one year's end to another in bad air, without chance of a change. They have no playgrounds; they amuse themselves with marbles and chuck-farthing, instead of cricket or hare-and-hounds; and if it were not for the wonderful instinct which leads all poor children of tender years to run under the feet of cab-horses whenever they can, I know not how they would learn to use their limbs with agility . . .

Whatever doubts people may entertain about the efficacy of natural selection, there can be none about artificial selection; and the breeder who should attempt to make, or keep up, a fine stock of pigs, or sheep, under the conditions to which the children of the poor are exposed, would be the laughing-stock even of the bucolic mind. Parliament has already done something in this direction by declining to be an accomplice in the asphyxiation of school children. It refuses to make any grant to a school in which the cubical contents of the school-room are inadequate to allow of proper respiration. I should like to see it make another step in the same direction, and either refuse to give a grant to a school in which physical training is not a part of the programme, or, at any rate, offer to pay upon such training. If something of the kind is not done, the English physique, which has been, and is still, on the whole, a grand one, will become as extinct as the dodo in the great towns.

And then the moral and intellectual effect of drill, as an introduction to, and aid of, all other sorts of training, must not be overlooked . . .

2. Next in order to physical training I put the instruction of children, and especially of girls, in the elements of household work and of domestic economy; in the first place for their own sakes, and in the second for that of their future employers.

Every one who knows anything of the life of the English poor is aware of the misery and waste caused by their want of knowledge of domestic economy, and by their lack of habits of frugality and method. I suppose it is no exaggeration to say that a poor Frenchwoman would make the money which the wife of a poor Englishman spends in food go twice as far, and at the same time turn out twice as palatable a dinner. Why Englishmen, who are so notoriously fond of good living, should be so helplessly incompetent in the art of cookery, is one of the great mysteries of nature; but from the varied abominations of the railway refreshment-rooms to the monotonous dinners of the poor, English feeding is either wasteful or nasty, or both . . .

3. But the boys and girls for whose education the School Boards have to provide, have not merely to discharge domestic duties, but each of them is a member of a social and political organisation of great complexity, and has, in future life, to fit himself into that organisation, or be crushed by it. To this end it is surely needful, not only that they should be made acquainted with the elementary laws of conduct, but that their affections should be trained, so as to love with all their hearts that conduct which tends to the attainment of the highest good for themselves and

their fellow men, and to hate with all their hearts that opposite course of action which is fraught with evil.

So far as the laws of conduct are determined by the intellect, I apprehend that they belong to science, and to that part of science which is called morality. But the engagement of the affections in favour of that particular kind of conduct which we call good, seems to me to be something quite beyond mere science. And I cannot but think that it, together with the awe and reverence, which have no kinship with base fear, but arise whenever one tries to pierce below the surface of things, whether they be material or spiritual, constitutes all that has any unchangeable reality in religion . . .

We are divided into two parties – the advocates of so-called 'religious' teaching on the one hand, and those of so-called 'secular' teaching on the other. And both parties seem to me to be not only hopelessly wrong, but in such a position that if either succeeded completely, it would discover, before many years were over, that it had made a great mistake and done serious evil to the cause of education.

For, leaving aside the more far-seeing minority on each side, what the 'religious' party is crying for is mere theology, under the name of religion; while the 'secularists' have unwisely and wrongfully admitted the assumption of their opponents, and demand the abolition of all 'religious' teaching, when they only want to be free of theology – Burning your ship to get rid of the cockroaches!

But my belief is, that no human being, and no society composed of human beings, ever did, or ever will, come to much, unless their conduct was governed and guided by the love of some ethical ideal . . .

Hence, when the great mass of the English people declare that they want to have the children in the elementary schools taught the Bible, and when it is plain from the terms of the Act, the debates in and out of Parliament, and especially the emphatic declarations of the Vice-President of the Council, that it was intended that such Bible-reading should be permitted, unless good cause for prohibiting it could be shown, I do not see what reason there is for opposing that wish. Certainly, I, individually, could with no shadow of consistency oppose the teaching of the children of other people to do that which my own children are taught to do. And, even if the reading the Bible were not, as I think it is, consonant with political reason and justice, and with a desire to act in the spirit of the education measure, I am disposed to think it might still be well to read that book in the elementary schools.

I have always been strongly in favour of secular education, in the sense of education without theology; but I must confess I have been no less seriously perplexed to know by what practical measures the religious feeling, which is the essential basis of conduct, was to be kept up, in the present utterly chaotic state of opinion on these matters, without the use of the Bible. The Pagan moralists lack life and colour, and even the noble Stoic, Marcus Antonius, is too high and refined for an ordinary child. Take the Bible as a whole; make the severest deductions which fair criticism can dictate for shortcomings and positive errors; eliminate, as a sensible lay-teacher would do, if left to himself, all that it is not desirable for children to occupy themselves with; and there still remains in this old literature a vast residuum of moral beauty and grandeur. And then consider the great historical fact that, for three centuries, this book has been woven into the life of all that is best and noblest in English history; that it has become the national epic of Britain, and is as familiar to noble and simple, from John-o'-Groat's House to Land's End, as Dante and Tasso once were to the Italians; that it is written in the noblest and purest English, and abounds in exquisite beauties of mere literary form; and, finally, that it forbids the veriest hind who never left his village to be ignorant of the existence of other countries and other civilisations, and of a great past, stretching back to the furthest limits of the oldest nations in the world. By the study of what other book could children be so much humanised?...

On the whole, then, I am in favour of reading the Bible, with such grammatical, geographical, and historical explanations by a lay-teacher as may be needful, with rigid exclusion of any further theological teaching than that contained in the Bible itself...

4. The intellectual training to be given in the elementary schools must of course, in the first place, consist in learning to use the means of acquiring knowledge, [of] reading, writing, and arithmetic; and it will be a great matter to teach reading so completely that the act shall have become easy and pleasant. If reading remains 'hard', that accomplishment will not be much resorted to for instruction, and still less for amusement – which last is one of its most valuable uses to hard-worked people. But along with a due proficiency in the use of the means of learning, a certain amount of knowledge, of intellectual discipline, and of artistic training should be conveyed in the elementary schools; and in this direction – for reasons which I am afraid to repeat, having urged them so often – I can conceive no subject-matter of education so appropriate and so important as the rudiments of physical [natural] science, with drawing, modelling, and singing...

It may be said that the scheme of education here sketched is too large to be effected in the time during which the children will remain at school; and, secondly, that even if this objection did not exist, it would cost too much.

I attach no importance whatever to the first objection until the experiment has been fairly tried. Considering how much catechism, lists of the kings of Israel, geography of Palestine, and the like, children are made to swallow now, I cannot believe there will be any difficulty in inducing them to go through the physical training, which is more than half play; or the instruction in household work, or in those duties to one another and to themselves, which will have a daily and hourly practical interest. That children take kindly to elementary science and art no one can doubt who has tried the experiment properly. And if Bible-reading is not accompanied by constraint and solemnity, as if it were a sacramental operation, I do not believe there is anything in which children take more pleasure. At least I know that some of the pleasantest recollections of my childhood are connected with the voluntary study of an ancient Bible which belonged to my grandmother. There were splendid pictures in it, to be sure; but I recollect little or nothing about them save a portrait of the high priest in his vestments. What come vividly back on my mind are remembrances of my delight in the histories of Joseph and of David; and of my keen appreciation of the chivalrous kindness of Abraham in his dealing with Lot. Like a sudden flash there returns back upon me, my utter scorn of the pettifogging meanness of Jacob, and my sympathetic grief over the heartbreaking lamentation of the cheated Esau, 'Hast thou not a blessing for me also, O my father?' And I see, as in a cloud, pictures of the grand phantasmagoria of the Book of Revelation . . .

And as to the second objection – costliness – the reply is, first, that the rate and the Parliamentary grant together ought to be enough, considering that science and art teaching is already provided for; and, secondly, that if they are not, it may be well for the educational parliament to consider what has become of those endowments which were originally intended to be devoted, more or less largely, to the education of the poor.

When the monasteries were spoiled, some of their
endowments were applied to the foundation of cathedrals;
and in all such cases it was ordered that a certain portion
of the endowment should be applied to the purposes of
education. How much is so applied? Is that which may
be so applied given to help the poor, who cannot pay for
education, or does it virtually subsidise the comparatively
rich, who can? How are Christ's Hospital and Alleyn's
foundation securing their right purposes, or how far are
they perverted into contrivances for affording relief to
the classes who can afford to pay for education? How –
But this paper is already too long, and, if I begin, I may
find it hard to stop asking questions of this kind, which
after all are worthy only of the lowest of Radicals.

Collected Essays, III, 374–403
Published in *The Contemporary Review*, XVI (December 1870), 1
Reprinted in T. H. Huxley, *Critiques and Addresses* (Macmillan,
1873)

ADMINISTRATIVE NIHILISM

(1871)

To me, and, as I trust, to the great majority of those whom I address, the great attempt to educate the people of England which has just been set afoot, is one of the most satisfactory and hopeful events in our modern history. But it is impossible, even if it were desirable, to shut our eyes to the fact, that there is a minority, not inconsiderable in numbers, nor deficient in supporters of weight and authority, in whose judgment all this legislation is a step in the wrong direction, false in principle, and consequently sure to produce evil in practice.

The arguments employed by these objectors are of two kinds. The first is what I will venture to term the caste argument; for, if logically carried out, it would end in the separation of the people of this country into castes, as permanent and as sharply defined, if not as numerous, as those of India. It is maintained that the whole fabric of society will be destroyed if the poor, as well as the rich, are educated; that anything like sound and good education will only make them discontented with their station and raise hopes which, in the great majority of cases, will be bitterly disappointed. It is said: There must be hewers of wood and drawers of water, scavengers and coalheavers, day labourers and domestic servants, or the work of society will come to a standstill. But, if you educate and refine everybody, nobody will be content to assume these functions, and all the world will want to be gentlemen and ladies.

One hears this argument most frequently from the representatives of the well-to-do middle class; and, coming from them, it strikes me as peculiarly inconsistent, as the one thing they admire, strive after, and advise their own children to do, is to get on in the world, and, if possible, rise out of the class in which they were born into that above them. Society needs grocers and merchants as much as it needs coalheavers; but if a merchant accumulates wealth and works his way to a baronetcy, or if the son of a greengrocer becomes a lord chancellor, or an archbishop, or, as a successful soldier, wins a peerage, all the world admires them; and looks with pride upon the social system which renders such achievements possible. Nobody suggests that there is anything wrong in their being discontented with their station; or that, in their cases society suffers by men of ability reaching the positions for which nature has fitted them . . .

A new-born infant does not come into the world labelled scavenger, shopkeeper, bishop or duke. One mass of red pulp is just like another to all outward appearance. And it is only by finding out what his faculties are good for, and seeking, not for the sake of gratifying a paltry vanity, but as the highest duty to himself and to his fellow-men, to put himself into the position in which they can attain their full development, that the man discovers his true station. That which is to be lamented, I fancy, is not that society should do its utmost to help capacity to ascend from the lower strata to the higher, but that it has no machinery by which to facilitate the descent of incapacity from the higher strata to the lower . . .

We have all known noble lords who would have been coachmen, or gamekeepers, or billiard-markers, if they had not been kept afloat by our social corks; we have all known men among the lowest ranks, of whom every one has said, 'what might not that man have become, if he had only had a little education?'

And who . . . can doubt that every man of high natural ability, who is both ignorant and miserable, is as great a danger to society as a rocket without a stick is to the people who fire it ? Misery is a match that never goes out; genius, as an explosive power, beats gunpowder hollow; and if knowledge, which should give that power guidance, is wanting, the chances are not small that the rocket will simply run a-muck among friends and foes. What gives force to the socialistic movement which is now stirring European society to its depths, but a determination on the part of the naturally able men among the proletariat, to put an end, somehow or other, to the misery and degradation in which a large proportion of their fellows are steeped ? . . .

Finally, as to the ladies and gentlemen question, all I can say is, would that every woman-child born into this world were trained to be a lady, and every man-child a gentleman ! But then I do not use those much-abused words by way of distinguishing people who wear fine clothes, and live in fine houses, and talk aristocratic slang, from those who go about in fustian, and live in back slums, and talk gutter slang. Some inborn plebeian blindness, in fact, prevents me from understanding what advantage the former have over the latter. I have never been able to understand why pigeon-shooting at Hurlingham should be refined and polite, while a rat-killing match in Whitechapel is low; or why 'What a lark' should be coarse, when one hears 'How awfully jolly' drop from the most refined lips twenty times in an evening . . .

Leaving the caste argument aside then, as inconsistent with the practice of those who employ it, as devoid of any justification in theory, and as utterly mischievous if its logical consequences were carried out, let us turn to the other class of objectors. To these opponents, the Education Act is only one of a number of pieces of legislation to which they object on principle; and they include under like condemnation the Vaccination Act, the Contagious

Diseases Act, and all other sanitary Acts; all attempts on the part of the State to prevent adulteration, or to regulate injurious trades; all legislative interference with anything that bears directly or indirectly on commerce, such as shipping, harbours, railways, roads, cab-fares, and the carriage of letters; and all attempts to promote the spread of knowledge by the establishment of teaching bodies, examining bodies, libraries, or museums, or by the sending out of scientific expeditions; all endeavours to advance art by the establishment of schools of design, or picture galleries; or by spending money upon an architectural public building when a brick box would answer the purpose. According to their views, not a shilling of public money must be bestowed upon a public park or pleasure-ground; not sixpence upon the relief of starvation, or the cure of disease. Those who hold these views support them by two lines of argument. They enforce them deductively by arguing from an assumed axiom, that the State has no right to do anything but protect its subjects from aggression. The State is simply a policeman, and its duty is neither more nor less than to prevent robbery and murder and enforce contracts. It is not to promote good, nor even to do anything to prevent evil, except by the enforcement of penalties upon those who have been guilty of obvious and tangible assaults upon purses or persons. And, according to this view, the proper form of government is neither a monarchy, an aristocracy, nor a democracy, but an *astynomocracy*, or police government. On the other hand, these views are supported *a posteriori*, by an induction from observation, which professes to show that whatever is done by a Government beyond these negative limits, is not only sure to be done badly, but to be done much worse than private enterprise would have done the same thing.

I am by no means clear as to the truth of the latter proposition. It is generally supported by statements which prove clearly enough that the State does a great many things very badly. But this is really beside the question. The State lives in a glass house; we see what it tries to do, and all its failures, partial or total, are made the most of. But private enterprise is sheltered under good opaque bricks and mortar. The public rarely knows what it tries to do, and only hears of failures when they are gross and patent to all the world. Who is to say how private enterprise would come out if it tried its hand at State work? . . . If continental bureaucracy and centralisation be fraught with multitudinous evils, surely English beadleocracy and parochial obstruction are not altogether lovely . . .

If my next-door neighbour chooses to have his drains in such a state as to create a poisonous atmosphere, which I breathe at the risk of typhoid and diphtheria, he restricts my just freedom to live just as much as if he went about with a pistol, threatening my life; if he is to be allowed to let his children go unvaccinated, he might as well be allowed to leave strychnine lozenges about in the way of mine; and if he brings them up untaught and untrained to earn their living, he is doing his best to restrict my freedom, by increasing the burden of taxation for the support of gaols and workhouses, which I have to pay.

The higher the state of civilisation, the more completely do the actions of one member of the social body influence all the rest, and the less possible is it for any one man to do a wrong thing without interfering, more or less, with the freedom of all his fellow-citizens. So that, even upon the narrowest view of the functions of the State, it must be admitted to have wider powers than the advocates of the police theory are disposed to admit . . .

Of late years, the belief in the efficacy of doing nothing . . . has acquired considerable popularity for several reasons. In the first place, men's speculative convictions have become less and less real; their tolerance is large because their belief is small ... In the second place, men have become largely absorbed in the mere accumulation of wealth; and as this is a matter in which the plainest and strongest form of self-interest is intensely concerned, science (in the shape of Political Economy) has readily demonstrated that self-interest may be safely left to find the best way of attaining its ends ... Thirdly, to the indifference generated by the absence of fixed beliefs, and to the confidence in the efficacy of *laissez-faire* ... there must be added that nobler and better reason for a profound distrust of legislative interference ... the just fear lest the end should be sacrificed to the means; lest freedom and variety should be drilled and disciplined out of human life in order that the great mill of the State should grind smoothly.

One of the profoundest of living English philosophers [Herbert Spencer], who is at the same time the most thoroughgoing and consistent of the champions of astynomocracy, has devoted a very able and ingenious essay to the drawing out of a comparison between the process by which men have advanced from the savage state to the highest civilisation, and that by which an animal passes from the condition of an almost shapeless and structureless germ, to that in which it exhibits a highly complicated structure and a corresponding diversity of powers...

But if the resemblances between the body physiological and the body politic are any indication, not only of what the latter is, and how it has become what it is, but of what it ought to be, and what it is tending to become, I cannot but think that the real force of the analogy is totally opposed to the negative view of State function...

The fact is that the sovereign power of the body thinks for the physiological organism, acts for it, and rules the individual components with a rod of iron. Even the blood-corpuscles can't hold a public meeting without being accused of 'congestion' – and the brain, like other despots whom we have known, calls out at once for the use of sharp steel against them . . . But, tempting as the opportunity is, I am not disposed to build up any argument in favour of my own case upon this analogy, curious, interesting, and in many respects close, as it is, for it takes no cognisance of certain profound and essential differences between the physiological and the political bodies . . .

It may be, that all the schemes of social organisation which have hitherto been propounded are impracticable follies. But if this be so the fact proves, not that the idea which underlies them is worthless, but only that the science of politics is in a very rudimentary and imperfect state. Politics, as a science, is not older than astronomy; but though the subject-matter of the latter is vastly less complex than that of the former, the theory of the moon's motions is not quite settled yet . . .

At present the State protects men in the possession and enjoyment of their property, and defines what that property is. The justification for its so doing is that its action promotes the good of the people. If it can be clearly proved that the abolition of [private] property would tend still more to promote the good of the people, the State will have the same justification for abolishing property that it now has for maintaining it . . .

Finally, with respect to the advancement of science and art. I have never yet had the good fortune to hear any valid reason alleged why that corporation of individuals we call the State may not do what voluntary effort fails in doing, either from want of intelligence or lack of will. And here it cannot be alleged that the action of the State is always hurtful. On the contrary, in every country in Europe, universities, public libraries, picture galleries, museums, and laboratories, have been established by the State, and have done infinite service to the intellectual and moral progress and the refinement of mankind...

To sum up: If the positive advancement of the peace, wealth, and the intellectual and moral development of its members, are objects which the Government, as the representative of the corporate authority of society, may justly strive after, in fulfilment of its end – the good of mankind; then it is clear that the Government may undertake to educate the people...

Collected Essays, i, 251–89

Address to Birmingham and Midland Institute, 9 October 1871

Published in *The Fortnightly Review*, n.s. xvi (1 November 1871), 525

Reprinted in T. H. Huxley, *Critiques and Addresses* (Macmillan, 1873)

ON THE HYPOTHESIS
THAT ANIMALS ARE AUTOMATA,
AND ITS HISTORY
(1874)

The first half of the seventeenth century is one of the great epochs of biological science ... the idea that the physical processes of life are capable of being explained in the same way as other physical phenomena, and, therefore, that the living body is a mechanism, was proved to be true for certain classes of vital actions; and ... this conception has not only successfully repelled every assault which has been made upon it, but has steadily grown in force and extent of application...

Modern physiology, aided by pathology, easily demonstrates that the brain is the seat of all forms of consciousness ... It proves, directly, that those states of consciousness which we call sensations are the immediate consequent of a change in the brain excited by the sensory nerves; and, on the well-known effects of injuries, of stimulants, and of narcotics, it bases the conclusion that thought and emotions are, in like manner, the consequents of physical antecedents...

That memory is dependent upon some condition of the brain is a fact established by many considerations – among the most important of which are the remarkable phenomena of aphasia. And that the condition of the brain on which memory depends, is largely determined by the repeated occurrence of that condition of its molecules, which gives rise to the idea of the thing remembered, is no less certain. Every boy who learns his lesson by repeating it exemplifies the fact...

It must be premised, that it is wholly impossible

absolutely to prove the presence or absence of consciousness in anything but one's own brain, though, by analogy,
we are justified in assuming its existence in other men.
Now if, by some accident ... the spinal cord is injured,
consciousness remains intact, except that the irritation of
parts below the injury is no longer represented by sensation.
On the other hand, pressure upon the anterior division of
the brain, or extensive injuries to it, abolish consciousness.
Hence, it is a highly probable conclusion, that consciousness in man depends upon the integrity of the anterior
division of the brain, while the middle and hinder divisions
of the brain, and the rest of the nervous centres, have
nothing to do with it. And it is further highly probable,
that what is true for man is true for other vertebrated
animals . . .

The doctrine of continuity is too well established for it
to be permissible to me to suppose that any complex natural
phenomenon comes into existence suddenly, and without
being preceded by simple modifications; and very strong
arguments would be needed to prove that such complex
phenomena as those of consciousness, first make their
appearance in man. We know, that, in the individual man,
consciousness grows from a dim glimmer to its full light,
whether we consider the infant advancing in years, or the
adult emerging from slumber and swoon. We know, further,
that the lower animals possess, though less developed,
that part of the brain which we have every reason to
believe to be the organ of consciousness in man; and as,
in other cases, function and organ are proportional, so
we have a right to conclude it is with the brain; and that
the brutes, though they may not possess our intensity of
consciousness, and though, from the absence of language,
they can have no trains of thoughts, but only trains of
feelings, yet have a consciousness which, more or less,
distinctly, foreshadows our own . . .

But though we may see reason to disagree with Descartes' hypothesis that brutes are unconscious machines, it does not follow that he was wrong in regarding them as automata. They may be more or less conscious, sensitive, automata; and the view that they are such conscious machines is that which is implicitly, or explicitly, adopted by most persons ... I believe that this generally accepted view is the best expression of the facts at present known...

Thus far I have strictly confined myself to the problem with which I proposed to deal at starting – the automatism of brutes. The question is, I believe, a perfectly open one, and I feel happy in running no risk of either Papal or Presbyterian condemnation for the views which I have ventured to put forward...

It will be said, that I mean that the conclusions deduced from the study of the brutes are applicable to man, and that the logical consequences of such application are fatalism, materialism, and atheism – whereupon the drums will beat the *pas de charge*...

It is quite true that, to the best of my judgment, the argumentation which applies to brutes holds equally good of men; and, therefore, that all states of consciousness in us, as in them, are immediately caused by molecular changes of the brain-substance. It seems to me that in men, as in brutes, there is no proof that any state of consciousness is the cause of change in the motion of the matter of the organism. If these positions are well based, it follows that our mental conditions are simply the symbols in consciousness of the changes which take place automatically in the organism; and that, to take an extreme illustration, the feeling we call volition is not the cause of a voluntary act, but the symbol of that state of the brain which is the immediate cause of that act. We are conscious automata, endowed with free will in the only intelligible sense of that much-abused term – inasmuch as in many respects we are able to do as we like – but none the less parts of the great series of causes and effects which, in unbroken continuity, composes that which is, and has been, and shall be – the sum of existence.

As to the logical consequences of this conviction of mine, I may be permitted to remark that logical consequences are the scarecrows of fools and the beacons of wise men. The only question which any wise man can ask himself, and which any honest man will ask himself, is whether a doctrine is true or false . . .

Collected Essays, I, 199–250

Address to the British Association for the Advancement of Science, Belfast, 1874

Summary in *Nature*, x (3 September 1874), 362

Published in *The Fortnightly Review*, XXII (XVI n.s.) (1 November 1874), 555

Reprinted in T. H. Huxley, *Science and Culture, and Other Essays* (Macmillan, 1881)

UNIVERSITIES: ACTUAL AND IDEAL

(1874)

Elected by the suffrages of your four Nations Rector of the ancient University of which you are scholars, I take the earliest opportunity which has presented itself since my restoration to health, of delivering the Address which, by long custom, is expected of the holder of my office...

When the proposal to nominate me for your Rector came, I was ... astonished ... And I fear that my acceptance must be taken as evidence that ... I have not yet done with soldiering ... Do not suppose, however, that I am sanguine enough to expect much to come of any poor efforts of mine. If your annals take any notice of my incumbency, I shall probably go down to posterity as the Rector who was always beaten. But if they add, as I think they will, that my defeats became victories in the hands of my successors, I shall be well content.

The scenes are shifting in the great theatre of the world... Change is in the air. It is whirling featherheads into all sorts of eccentric orbits, and filling the steadiest with a sense of insecurity. It insists on reopening all questions and asking all institutions, however venerable, by what right they exist, and whether they are, or are not, in harmony with the real or supposed wants of mankind. And it is remarkable that these searching inquiries are not so much forced on institutions from without, as developed from within. Consummate scholars question the value of learning; priests contemn dogma; and women turn their backs upon man's ideal of perfect womanhood...

If there be a type of stability in this world, one would be

inclined to look for it in the old Universities of England. But ... things are moving so fast in Oxford and Cambridge, that, for my part, I rejoiced when the Royal Commission, of which I am a member, had finished and presented the Report which related to these Universities; for we should have looked like mere plagiarists, if, in consequence of a little longer delay in issuing it, all the measures of reform we proposed had been anticipated by the spontaneous action of the Universities themselves...

The Scottish Universities, like the English, have diverged widely enough from their primitive model; but I cannot help thinking that the northern form has remained more faithful to its original, not only in constitution, but, what is more to the purpose, in view of the cry for change, in the practical application of the endowments connected with it.

In Aberdeen, these endowments are numerous, but so small that, taken altogether, they are not equal to the revenue of a single third-rate English college. They are scholarships, not fellowships; aids to do work – not rewards for such work as it lies within the reach of an ordinary, or even an extraordinary, young man to do. You do not think that passing a respectable examination is a fair equivalent for an income, such as many a grey-headed veteran, or clergyman would envy; and which is larger than the endowment of many Regius chairs. You do not care to make your University a school of manners for the rich; of sports for the athletic; or a hot-bed of high fed, hypercritical refinement, more destructive to vigour and originality than are starvation and oppression...

When I think of the host of pleasant, moneyed, well-bred young gentlemen, who do a little learning and much boating by Cam and Isis, the vision is a pleasant one; and, as a patriot, I rejoice that the youth of the upper and richer classes of the nation receive a wholesome and a manly training, however small may be the modicum of knowledge they gather, in the intervals of this, their serious business. I admit, to the full, the social and political value of that training. But, when I proceed to consider that these young men may be said to represent the great bulk of what the Colleges have to show for their enormous wealth . . . I feel inclined to ask, whether the rate-in-aid of the education of the wealthy and professional classes, thus levied on the resources of the community, is not, after all, a little heavy ? And, still further, I am tempted to inquire what has become of the indigent scholars, the sons of the masses of the people whose daily labour just suffices to meet their daily wants, for whose benefit these rich foundations were largely, if not mainly, instituted ? . . . And when I turn from this picture to the no less real vision of many a brave and frugal Scotch boy, spending his summer in hard manual labour, that he may have the privilege of wending his way in autumn to this University . . . determined to wring knowledge from the hard hands of penury . . . I cannot but think that . . . the spirit of reform has so much to do on the other side of the Border, that it may be long before he has leisure to look this way.

As compared with other actual Universities, then, Aberdeen, may, perhaps, be well satisfied with itself. But . . . I ask you to consider awhile, how this actual good stands related to that ideal better, towards which both men and institutions must progress, if they would not retrograde.

In an ideal University, as I conceive it, a man should be able to obtain instruction in all forms of knowledge, and discipline in the use of all the methods by which knowledge is obtained. In such a University, the force of living example should fire the student with a noble ambition to emulate the learning of learned men, and to follow in the footsteps of the explorers of new fields of knowledge. And the very air he breathes should be charged with that enthusiasm for truth, that fanaticism of veracity, which is a greater possession than much learning; a nobler gift than the power of increasing knowledge; by so much greater and nobler than these, as the moral nature of man is greater than the intellectual; for veracity is the heart of morality.

But the man who is all morality and intellect, although he may be good and even great, is, after all, only half a man. There is beauty in the moral world and in the intellectual world; but there is also a beauty which is neither moral nor intellectual – the beauty of the world of Art. There are men who are devoid of the power of seeing it, as there are men who are born deaf and blind, and the loss of those, as of these, is simply infinite. There are others in whom it is an overpowering passion; happy men, born with the productive, or at lowest, the appreciative, genius of the Artist. But, in the mass of mankind, the Aesthetic faculty, like the reasoning power and the moral sense, needs to be roused, directed, and cultivated; and I know not why the development of that side of his nature, through which man has access to a perennial spring of ennobling pleasure, should be omitted from any comprehensive scheme of University education ... If there are Doctors of Music, why should there be no Masters of Painting, of Sculpture, of Architecture? I should like to see Professors of the Fine Arts in every University ...

I just now expressed the opinion that, in our ideal University, a man should be able to obtain instruction in all forms of knowledge. Now, by 'forms of knowledge' I mean the great classes of things knowable; of which the first, in logical, though not in natural, order is knowledge relating to the scope and limits of the mental faculties of man ... Logic and part of Psychology [and] ... Metaphysics. A second class comprehends all that knowledge

10

which relates to man's welfare, so far as it is determined by his own acts, or what we call his conduct. It answers to Moral and Religious philosophy . . . A third class embraces knowledge of the phaenomena of the Universe . . . and of the rules which those phaenomena are observed to follow . . . This is what ought to be called Natural Science . . . and it includes all exact knowledge of natural fact, whether Mathematical, Physical, Biological, or Social.

Kant has said that the ultimate object of all knowledge is to give replies to these three questions: What can I do? What ought I to do? What may I hope for? The forms of knowledge which I have enumerated, should furnish such replies as are within human reach, to the first and second of these questions. While to the third, perhaps the wisest answer is, 'Do what you can to do what you ought, and leave hoping and fearing alone'.

If this be a just and an exhaustive classification of the forms of knowledge, no question as to their relative importance, or as to the superiority of one to the other, can be seriously raised . . . it is absurd to ask whether it is more important to know the limits of one's powers; or the ends for which they ought to be exerted; or the conditions under which they must be exerted. One may as well inquire which of the terms of a Rule of Three sum one ought to know, in order to get a trustworthy result . . .

The founders of Universities held the theory that the Scriptures and Aristotle taken together, the latter being limited by the former, contained all knowledge worth having, and that the business of philosophy was to interpret and co-ordinate these two. I imagine that in the twelfth century this was a very fair conclusion from known facts. Nowhere in the world, in those days, was there such an encyclopaedia of knowledge of all three classes, as is to be found in those writings . . .

Well, this great system had its day, and then it was

sapped and mined by two influences. The first was the study of classical literature, which familiarised men with methods of philosophising; with conceptions of the highest Good; with ideas of the order of Nature; with notions of Literary and Historical Criticism; and, above all, with visions of Art, of . . . such grandeur and beauty that they ceased to think of any other. They were as men who had kissed the Fairy Queen . . . Cardinals were more familiar with Virgil than with Isaiah; and Popes laboured, with great success, to re-paganise Rome.

The second influence was the slow, but sure, growth of the physical [natural] sciences . . . to the certainty of which no authority could add, or take away, one jot or tittle, and to which the tradition of a thousand years was as insignificant as the hearsay of yesterday. To the scholastic system, the study of classical literature might be inconvenient and distracting, but it was possible to hope that it could be kept within bounds. Physical science, on the other hand, was an irreconcilable enemy, to be excluded at all hazards . . .

But it is only fair to the Scottish Universities to point out that they have long understood the value of Science as a branch of general education. I observe, with the greatest satisfaction, that candidates for the degree of Master of Arts in this University are required to have a knowledge, not only of Mental and Moral Philosophy, and of Mathematics and Natural Philosophy, but of Natural History . . . I do not know what the requirements of your examiners may be, but I sincerely trust that they are not satisfied with a mere book knowledge of these matters. For my own part I would not raise a finger, if I could thereby introduce mere book work in science into every Arts curriculum in the country . . .

A little while ago, I ventured to hint a doubt as to the perfection of some of the arrangements in the ancient

Universities of England; but ... within the last twenty years, Oxford alone has sunk more than a hundred and twenty thousand pounds in building and furnishing Physical, Chemical, and Physiological Laboratories, and a magnificent Museum, arranged with an almost luxurious regard for the needs of the student. Cambridge, less rich, but aided by the munificence of her Chancellor, is taking the same course; and in a few years, it will be for no lack of the means and appliances of sound teaching, if the mass of English University men remain in their present state of barbarous ignorance of even the rudiments of scientific culture.

Yet another step needs to be made before Science can be said to have taken its proper place in the Universities. That is its recognition as a Faculty, or branch of study demanding recognition and special organisation, on account of its bearing on the wants of mankind ... I would urge that a thorough study of Human physiology is, in itself, an education broader and more comprehensive than much that passes under that name. There is no side of the intellect which it does not call into play, no region of human knowledge into which either its roots, or its branches, do not extend; like the Atlantic between the Old and the New Worlds, its waves wash the shores of the two worlds of matter and of mind; its tributary streams flow from both; through its waters, as yet unfurrowed by the keel of any Columbus, lies the road, if such there be, from the one to the other; far away from that North-West Passage of mere speculation, in which so many brave souls have been hopelessly frozen up ...

I think that sound and practical instruction in the elementary facts and broad principles of Biology should form part of the Arts Curriculum: and ... I have no sort of doubt that in view of the relation of Physical [Natural] Science to the practical life of the present day, it has the same right as Theology, Law, and Medicine, to a Faculty of its own in which men shall be trained to be professional men of science ... The establishment of such a Faculty would have the additional advantage of providing, in some measure, for one of the greatest wants of our time and country. I mean the proper support and encouragement of original research...

Great schemes for the Endowment of Research have been proposed. It has been suggested, that Laboratories for all branches of Physical Science, provided with every apparatus needed by the investigator, shall be established by the State: and shall be accessible, under due conditions and regulations, to all properly qualified persons. I see no objection to the principle of such a proposal ... To my mind, the difficulty in the way of such schemes is not theoretical, but practical ... I do not say that these difficulties may not be overcome, but their gravity is not to be lightly estimated.

In the meanwhile, there is one step in the direction of the endowment of research which is free from such objections. It is possible to place the scientific enquirer in a position in which he shall have ample leisure and opportunity for original work, and yet shall give a fair and tangible equivalent for those privileges. The establishment of a Faculty of Science in every University, implies that of a corresponding number of Professorial chairs, the incumbents of which need not be so burdened with teaching as to deprive them of ample leisure for original work. I do not think that it is any impediment to an original investigator to have to devote a moderate portion of his time to lecturing, or superintending practical instruction. On the contrary, I think it may be, and often is, a benefit to be obliged to take a comprehensive survey of your subject; or to bring your results to a point, and give them, as it were, a tangible objective existence. The besetting sins of the investigator are two: the one is the desire to put aside a subject, the general bearings of which he has mastered himself, and pass on to something which has the attraction of novelty; and the other, the desire for too much perfection, which leads him to

> Add and alter many times,
> Till all be ripe and rotten;

to spend the energies which should be reserved for action in whitening the decks and polishing the guns. The obligation to produce results for the instruction of others, seems to me to be a more effectual check on these tendencies than even the love of usefulness or the ambition for fame...

Examination – thorough, searching examination – is an indispensable accompaniment of teaching; but I am almost inclined to commit myself to the very heterodox proposition that it is a necessary evil. I am a very old Examiner ... from the boys and girls of elementary schools to the candidates for Honours and Fellowships in the Universities ... but my admiration for the existing system of examination and its products, does not wax warmer as I see more of it. Examination, like fire, is a good servant, but a bad master; and there seems to me to be some danger of its becoming our master. I by no means stand alone in this opinion. Experienced friends of mine do not hesitate to say that students whose careers they watch, appear to them to become deteriorated by the constant effort to pass this or that examination ... They work to pass, not to know; and outraged Science takes her revenge. They do pass, and they don't know...

Again there is a fallacy about Examiners. It is commonly supposed that any one who knows a subject is competent to teach it; and no one seems to doubt that any one who knows a subject is competent to examine in it. I believe both these opinions to be serious mistakes: the latter, perhaps, the more serious of the two. In the first place, I do not believe that any one who is not, or has not been, a teacher is really qualified to examine advanced students. And in the second place, Examination is an Art, and a difficult one, which has to be learned like all other arts.

Beginners always set too difficult questions – partly because they are afraid of being suspected of ignorance if they set easy ones, and partly from not understanding their business. Suppose that you want to test the relative physical strength of a score of young men. You do not put a hundredweight down before them, and tell each to swing it round. If you do, half of them won't be able to lift it at all, and only one or two will be able to perform the task. You must give them half a hundredweight, and see how they manoeuvre that, if you want to form any estimate of the muscular strength of each. So, a practised Examiner will seek for information respecting the mental vigour and training of candidates from the way in which they deal with questions easy enough to let reason, memory, and method have free play.

No doubt, a great deal is to be done by the careful selection of Examiners, and by the copious introduction of practical work, to remove the evils inseparable from examination; but, under the best of circumstances, I believe that examination will remain but an imperfect test of knowledge, and a still more imperfect test of capacity, while it tells next to nothing about a man's power as an investigator . . .

Thus far, I have endeavoured to lay before you, in a too brief and imperfect manner, my views respecting the teaching half – the Magistri and Regentes – of the University of the Future. Now let me turn to the learning half – the Scholares.

If the Universities are to be the sanctuaries of the highest culture of the country, those who would enter that sanctuary must not come with unwashed hands. If the good seed is to yield its hundredfold harvest, it must not be scattered amidst the stones of ignorance, or the tares of undisciplined indolence and wantonness. On the contrary, the soil must have been carefully prepared, and the Professor should find that the operations of clod-crushing, draining, and weeding, and even a good deal of planting, have been done by the Schoolmaster.

That is exactly what the Professor does not find in any University in the three Kingdoms that I can hear of – the reason of which state of things lies in the extremely faulty organisation of the majority of secondary schools. Students come to the Universities ill-prepared in classics and mathematics, not at all prepared in anything else; and half their time is spent in learning that which they ought to have known when they came . . .

You are not responsible for this anomalous state of affairs now; but, as you pass into active life and acquire the political influence to which your education and your position should entitle you, you will become responsible for it, unless each in his sphere does his best to alter it, by insisting on the improvement of secondary schools.

Your present responsibility is of another, though not less serious, kind. Institutions do not make men, any more than organisation makes life; and even the ideal University we have been dreaming about will be but a superior piece of mechanism, unless each student strive after the ideal of the Scholar. And that ideal, it seems to me, has never been better embodied than by the great Poet [Goethe], who, though lapped in luxury, the favourite of a Court, and the idol of his countrymen, remained through all the length of his honoured years a Scholar in Art, in Science, and in Life.

Wouldst shape a noble life ? Then cast
No backward glances towards the past :
And though somewhat be lost and gone,
Yet do thou act as one new-born.
What each day needs, that shalt thou ask ;
Each day will set its proper task.
Give others' work just share of praise ;
Not of thine own the merits raise.
Beware no fellow man thou hate :
And so in God's hands leave thy fate.

Collected Essays, III, 189–234
Rectorial Address to University of Aberdeen, 27 February 1874
Summary in *The Scotsman* (28 February 1874)
Published in *The Contemporary Review*, XXIII (March 1874), 657
Reprinted in T. H. Huxley, *Science and Culture, and Other
    Essays* (Macmillan, 1881)

ADDRESS ON UNIVERSITY EDUCATION

(1876)

The actual work of the University founded in this city by the well-considered munificence of Johns Hopkins commences tomorrow, and among the many marks of confidence and goodwill which have been bestowed upon me in the United States, there is none which I value more highly than that conferred by the authorities of the University when they invited me to deliver an address on such an occasion . . .

Under one aspect a university is a particular kind of educational institution, and the views which we may take of the proper nature of a university are corollaries from those which we hold respecting education in general. I think it must be admitted that the school should prepare for the university, and that the university should crown the edifice, the foundations of which are laid in the school. University education should not be something distinct from elementary education, but should be the natural outgrowth and development of the latter . . .

The university can add no new departments of knowledge, can offer no new fields of mental activity; but what it can do is to intensify and specialise the instruction in each department. Thus literature and philology, represented in the elementary school by English alone, in the university will extend over the ancient and modern languages. History, which, like charity, best begins at home, but, like charity, should not end there, will ramify into anthropology, archaeology, political history, and geography, with the history of the growth of the human mind and of its products in the shape of philosophy, science, and art. And the university will present to the student libraries, museums of antiquities, collections of coins, and the like, which will efficiently subserve these studies. Instruction in the elements of social economy, a most essential, but hitherto sadly-neglected part of elementary education, will develop in the university into political economy, sociology, and law. Physical science will have its great divisions of physical geography, with geology and astronomy; physics; chemistry and biology; represented not merely by professors and their lectures but by laboratories, in which the students, under guidance of demonstrators, will work out facts for themselves and come into that direct contact with reality which constitutes the fundamental distinction of scientific education. Mathematics will soar into its highest regions; while the high peaks of philosophy may be scaled by those whose aptitude for abstract thought has been awakened by elementary logic. Finally, schools of pictorial and plastic art, of architecture, and of music, will offer a thorough discipline in the principles and practice of art to those in whom lies nascent the rare faculty of aesthetic representation, or the still rarer powers of creative genius.

The primary school and the university are the alpha and omega of education...

My own feeling is distinctly against any absolute and defined preliminary examination, the passing of which shall be an essential condition of admission to the university. I would admit to the university any one who could be reasonably expected to profit by the instruction offered to him; and I should be inclined, on the whole, to test the fitness of the student, not by examination before he enters the University, but at the end of his first term of study. If, on examination in the branches of knowledge to which he has devoted himself, he show himself deficient in industry or in capacity, it will be best for the university and best for himself, to prevent him from pursuing a vocation for which he is obviously unfit...

One half of the Johns Hopkins bequest is devoted to the establishment of a hospital, and it was the desire of the testator that the university and the hospital should co-operate in the promotion of medical education...

What is the object of medical education? It is to enable the practitioner, on the one hand, to prevent disease by his knowledge of hygiene; on the other hand, to divine its nature, and to alleviate or cure it, by his knowledge of pathology, therapeutics, and practical medicine. That is his business in life, and if he has not a thorough and practical knowledge of the conditions of health, of the causes which tend to the establishment of disease, of the meaning of symptoms, and of the uses of medicines and operative appliances, he is incompetent, even if he were the best anatomist, or physiologist, or chemist, that ever took a gold medal or won a prize certificate ... To understand the nature of disease we must understand health, and the understanding of the healthy body means the having a knowledge of its structure and of the way in which its manifold actions are performed, which is what is technically termed human anatomy and human physiology...

Consider, in addition, that the medical practitioner may be called upon, at any moment, to give evidence in a court of justice in a criminal case; and that it is therefore well that he should know something of the laws of evidence, and of what we call medical jurisprudence. On a medical certificate, a man may be taken from his home and from his business and confined in a lunatic asylum; surely, therefore, it is desirable that the medical practitioner should have some rational and clear conceptions as to the nature and symptoms of mental disease. Bearing in mind all these requirements of medical education, you will admit that the burden on the young aspirant for the medical profession is somewhat of the heaviest, and that it needs some care to prevent his intellectual back from being broken...

Let it not be supposed that I am proposing to narrow medical education, or, as the cry is, to lower the standard of the profession. Depend upon it there is only one way of really ennobling any calling, and that is to make those who pursue it real masters of their craft, men who can truly do that which they profess to be able to do, and which they are credited with being able to do by the public. And there is no position so ignoble as that of the so-called 'liberally-educated practitioner', who may be able to read Galen in the original; who knows all the plants, from the cedar of Lebanon to the hyssop upon the wall; but who finds himself, with the issues of life and death in his hands, ignorant, blundering, and bewildered, because of his ignorance of the essential and fundamental truths upon which practice must be based...

In England within my recollection, it was the practice to require of the medical student attendance on lectures upon the most diverse topics during three years; so that it often happened that he would have to listen, in the course of a day, to four or five lectures upon totally different subjects, in addition to the hours given to dissection and to hospital practice: and he was required to keep all the knowledge he could pick up, in this distracting fashion, at examination point, until, at the end of three years, he was set down to a table and questioned pell-mell upon all the different matters with which he had been striving to make acquaintance. A worse system and one more calculated to obstruct the acquisition of sound knowledge and to give full play to the 'crammer' and the 'grinder' could hardly have been devised by human ingenuity...

Those who are occupied in intellectual work, will, I

think, agree with me that it is important, not so much to know a thing, as to have known it, and known it thoroughly. If you have once known a thing in this way it is easy to renew your knowledge when you have forgotten it; and when you begin to take the subject up again, it slides back upon the familiar grooves with great facility . . .

I rejoice to observe that the encouragement of research occupies so prominent a place in your official documents, and in the wise and liberal inaugural address of your president. This subject of the encouragement, or, as it is sometimes called, the endowment of research, has of late years greatly exercised the minds of men in England. It was one of the main topics of discussion by the members of the Royal Commission of whom I was one, and who not long since issued their report, after five years' labour. Many seem to think that this question is mainly one of money; that you can go into the market and buy research, and that supply will follow demand, as in the ordinary course of commerce. This view does not commend itself to my mind. I know of no more difficult practical problem than the discovery of a method of encouraging and supporting the original investigator without opening the door to nepotism and jobbery . . .

I constantly hear Americans speak of the charm which our old mother country has for them, of the delight with which they wander through the streets of ancient towns, or climb the battlements of mediaeval strongholds, the names of which are indissolubly associated with the great epochs of that noble literature which is our common inheritance; or with the blood-stained steps of that secular progress, by which the descendants of the savage Britons and of the wild pirates of the North Sea have become converted into warriors of order and champions of peaceful freedom, exhausting what still remains of the old Berserk

spirit in subduing nature, and turning the wilderness into
a garden. But anticipation has no less charm than retro-
spect, and to an Englishman landing upon your shores for
the first time, travelling for hundreds of miles through
strings of great and well-ordered cities, seeing your enormous actual, and almost infinite potential, wealth in all
commodities, and in the energy and ability which turn
wealth to account, there is something sublime in the vista
of the future. Do not suppose that I am pandering to what
is commonly understood by national pride. I cannot say
that I am in the slightest degree impressed by your bigness,
or your material resources, as such. Size is not grandeur,
and territory does not make a nation. The great issue,
about which hangs a true sublimity, and the terror of
overhanging fate, is what are you going to do with all these
things? What is to be the end to which these are to be the
means? You are making a novel experiment in politics on
the greatest scale which the world has yet seen. Forty
millions at your first centenary, it is reasonably to be
expected that, at the second, these states will be occupied
by two hundred millions of English-speaking people,
spread over an area as large as that of Europe, and with
climates and interests as diverse as those of Spain and
Scandinavia, England and Russia. You and your descendants have to ascertain whether this great mass will hold
together under the forms of a republic, and the despotic
reality of universal suffrage; whether state rights will hold
out against centralisation, without separation; whether
centralisation will get the better, without actual or dis-
guised monarchy; whether shifting corruption is better
than a permanent bureaucracy; and as population thickens
in your great cities, and the pressure of want is felt, the
gaunt spectre of pauperism will stalk among you, and
communism and socialism will claim to be heard. Truly
America has a great future before her; great in toil, in care,

and in responsibility; great in true glory if she be guided in wisdom and righteousness; great in shame if she fail. I cannot understand why other nations should envy you, or be blind to the fact that it is for the highest interest of mankind that you should succeed; but the one condition of success, your sole safeguard, is the moral worth and intellectual clearness of the individual citizen. Education cannot give these, but it may cherish them and bring them to the front in whatever station of society they are to be found; and the universities ought to be, and may be, the fortresses of the higher life of the nation.

May the university which commences its practical activity to-morrow abundantly fulfil its high purpose; may its renown as a seat of true learning, a centre of free inquiry, a focus of intellectual light, increase year by year, until men wander hither from all parts of the earth, as of old they sought Bologna, or Paris, or Oxford.

And it is pleasant to me to fancy that, among the English students who are drawn to you at that time, there may linger a dim tradition that a countryman of theirs was permitted to address you as he has done to-day, and to feel as if your hopes were his hopes and your success his joy.

Collected Essays, III, 235–61

Address at opening of Johns Hopkins University, 12 September 1876

Published in T. H. Huxley, *American Addresses* (Macmillan, 1877)

ON THE STUDY OF BIOLOGY

(1876)

It is my duty to-night to speak about the study of Biology ... I shall ... endeavour to give you some answer to these four questions – what Biology is; why it should be studied; how it should be studied; and when it should be studied...

At the revival of learning, knowledge was divided into two kinds – the knowledge of nature [Natural History] and the knowledge of man [Civil History] ... As time went on, and the various branches of human knowledge became more distinctly developed and separated from one another, it was found that some were much more susceptible of precise mathematical treatment than others ... [and these] came to be spoken of as 'natural philosophy' ... Under these circumstances the old name of 'Natural History' stuck by the residuum ... physical geography, geology, mineralogy, the history of plants, and the history of animals...

But as science made the marvellous progress which it did make at the latter end of the last and the beginning of the present century, thinking men began to discern that under this title of 'Natural History' there were included very heterogenous constituents ... and, further as knowledge advanced, it became clear that there was a great analogy, a very close alliance, between ... botany and zoology ... Therefore, it is not wonderful that, at the beginning of the present century, in two different countries, and so far as I know, without any intercommunication, two famous men [Lamarck and Treviranus] clearly conceived the notion of uniting the sciences which deal with living matter into one whole, and of dealing with them as one discipline...

'Biologie', from the two Greek words which signify a discourse upon life and living things . . .

Now that we have arrived at the origin of this word 'Biology', the next point to consider is: What ground does it cover? I have said that in its strict technical sense, it denotes all the phenomena which are exhibited by living things, as distinguished from those which are not living; but while that is all very well, so long as we confine ourselves to the lower animals and to plants, it lands us in considerable difficulties when we reach the higher forms of living things. For . . . if our definition is to be interpreted strictly, we must include man and all his ways and works under the head of Biology; in which case, we should find that psychology, politics and political economy would be absorbed into the province of Biology . . . There has been a sort of practical convention by which we give up to a different branch of science what Bacon and Hobbes would have called 'Civil History' . . . but . . . you should not be surprised if it occasionally happens that you see a biologist apparently trespassing in the region of philosophy or politics; or meddling with human education; because, after all, that is a part of his kingdom which he has only voluntarily forsaken . . .

I turn to my second question, which is – Why should we study Biology? Possibly the time may come when that will seem a very odd question . . .

I judge the value of human pursuits by their bearing upon human interests; in other words, by their utility; but I should like that we should quite clearly understand what it is that we mean by this word 'utility'. In an Englishman's mouth it generally means that by which we get pudding or praise, or both. I have no doubt that is one meaning of the word utility, but it by no means includes all I mean by utility. I think that knowledge of every kind is useful in proportion as it tends to give people right ideas

... to remove wrong ideas ... And inasmuch as, whatever practical people may say, this world is, after all, absolutely governed by ideas ... it is a matter of the very greatest importance that our theories ... should be as far as possible true ... It is not only in the coarser, practical sense of the word 'utility', but in this higher and broader sense, that I measure the value of the study of biology by its utility ... For example, most of us attach great importance to the conception which we entertain of the position of man in this universe and his relation to the rest of nature. We have almost all been told, and most of us hold by the tradition, that man occupies an isolated and peculiar position in nature; that though he is in the world he is not of the world; that his relations to things about him are of a remote character; that his origin is recent, his duration likely to be short, and that he is the great central figure round which other things in this world revolve. But this is not what the biologist tells us...

If what the biologist tells us is true, it will be needful to get rid of our erroneous conceptions of man, and of his place in nature, and to substitute right ones for them. But it is impossible to form any judgment as to whether the biologists are right or wrong, unless we are able to appreciate the nature of the arguments which they have to offer.

One would almost think this to be a self-evident proposition. I wonder what a scholar would say to the man who should undertake to criticise a difficult passage in a Greek play, but who obviously had not acquainted himself with the rudiments of Greek grammar. And yet, before giving positive opinions about these high questions of Biology, people not only do not seem to think it necessary to be acquainted with the grammar of the subject, but they have not even mastered the alphabet. You find criticism and denunciation showered about by persons who ... have not even reached that stage of emergence from ignorance in which the knowledge that such a discipline is necessary dawns upon the mind . . .

Granted that Biology is something worth studying, what is the best way of studying it ? . . . It has now long been recognised that, if a man wishes to be a chemist . . . he should actually perform the fundamental experiments in the laboratory for himself, and thus learn exactly what the words which he finds in his books and hears from his teachers, mean. If he does not do so, he may read till the crack of doom, but he will never know much about chemistry . . . The same thing is true in Biology. Nobody will ever know anything about Biology except in a dilettante 'paper-philosopher' way, who contents himself with reading books on botany, zoology, and the like; and the reason of this is simple and easy to understand. It is that all language is merely symbolical of the things of which it treats; the more complicated the things, the more bare is the symbol, and the more its verbal definition requires to be supplemented by the information derived directly from the handling, and the seeing, and the touching of the thing symbolised: – that is really what is at the bottom of the whole matter. It is plain common sense, as all truth, in the long run, is only common sense clarified . . .

I lecture to a class of students daily for about four-and-a-half months, and my class have, of course, their text-books; but the essential part of the whole teaching . . . is a laboratory for practical work . . . We have tables properly arranged in regard to light, microscopes, and dissecting instruments, and we work through the structure of a certain number of animals and plants . . . The purpose of this course is not to make skilled dissectors, but to give every student a clear and definite conception, by means of sense-images, of the characteristic structure of each of the leading modifications of the animal kingdom . . . And it then becomes possible for him to read with profit;

because every time he meets with the name of a structure he has a definite image in his mind of what the name means in the particular creature he is reading about, and therefore the reading is not mere reading . . .

Lastly comes the question as to when biological study may best be pursued . . . I am perfectly certain that it can be carried out [in the ordinary schools] with ease, and not only with ease, but with very considerable profit to those who are taught; but then such instruction must be adapted to the minds and needs of the scholars . . . I sometimes fancy the spirit of the old classical system has entered into the new scientific system, in which case I would much rather that any pretence at scientific teaching were abolished altogether. What really has to be done is to get into the young mind some notion of what animal and vegetable life is. In this matter, you have to consider practical convenience as well as other things. There are difficulties in the way of a lot of boys making messes with slugs and snails . . . But there is a very convenient and handy animal which everybody has at hand, and that is himself; and it is a very easy and simple matter to obtain common plants. Hence the general truths of anatomy and physiology can be taught to young people in a very real fashion by dealing with the broad facts of human structure. Such viscera as they cannot very well examine in themselves, such as hearts, lungs, and livers, may be obtained from the nearest butcher's shop. In respect to teaching something about the biology of plants, there is no practical difficulty, because almost any of the common plants will do, and plants do not make a mess – at least they do not make an unpleasant mess; so that, in my judgment the best form of Biology for teaching to very young people is elementary human physiology on the one hand, and the elements of botany on the other; beyond that I do not think it will be feasible to advance for some time to come . . .

Collected Essays, III, 262–93

Address at inauguration of loan collection, South Kensington Museum (under the title, 'The Systematic Study of Biology'), 16 December 1876

Summary in *The Times* (18 December 1876)

Published in *Nature*, XV (11 January 1877), 219

Reprinted in *American Naturalist*, XI (1877), 210 and in *Popular Science Monthly*, X (1877), 527

ON ELEMENTARY INSTRUCTION
IN PHYSIOLOGY

(1877)

The chief ground upon which I venture to recommend . . . the teaching of elementary physiology . . . is, that a knowledge of even the elements of this subject . . . prepare[s] the mind to receive instruction from sanitary science . . . The elementary and fundamental truths can be made clear to a child . . .

The subject of study is always at hand, in one's self. The principal constituents of the skeleton, and the changes of form of contracting muscles, may be felt through one's own skin. The beating of one's heart, and its connection with the pulse, may be noted; the influence of the valves of one's own veins may be shown; the movements of respiration may be observed; while the wonderful phenomena of sensation afford an endless field for curious and interesting self-study. The prick of a needle will yield, in a drop of one's own blood, material for microscopic observation of phenomena which lie at the foundation of all biological conceptions; and a cold, with its concomitant coughing and sneezing, may prove the sweet uses of adversity by helping one to a clear conception of what is meant by 'reflex action'.

Of course there is a limit to this physiological self-examination. But . . . The saying that a little knowledge is a dangerous thing is, to my mind, a very dangerous adage. If knowledge is real and genuine, I do not believe that it is other than a very valuable possession however infinitesimal its quantity may be. Indeed, if a little knowledge is dangerous, where is the man who has so much as to be out of danger? . . .

Collected Essays, III, 294–302

Address at Society of Arts' first Domestic Economy Congress,
Birmingham, 17 July 1877

Summary in *Journal of Society of Arts*, xxv (20 July 1877), 831

Published in T. H. Huxley, *Science and Culture, and Other Essays*
(Macmillan, 1881)

TECHNICAL EDUCATION

(1877)

'Technical education', in the sense in which the term is ordinarily used, and in which I am now employing it, means that sort of education which is specially adapted to the needs of men whose business in life it is to pursue some kind of handicraft ... I am, and have been, any time these thirty years, a man who works with his hands – a handicraftsman. I do not say this in the broadly metaphorical sense in which fine gentlemen, with all the delicacy of Agag about them, trip to the hustings about election time, and protest that they too are working men. I really mean my words to be taken in their direct, literal, and straightforward sense ...

Indeed, it has struck me that one of the grounds of that sympathy between the handicraftsmen of this country and the men of science, by which it has so often been my good fortune to profit, may, perhaps, lie here. You feel and we feel that, among the so-called learned folks, we alone are brought into contact with tangible facts in the way that you are ... [and] we, like you, have to get our work done in a region where little avails, if the power of dealing with practical tangible facts is wanting. You know that clever talk touching joinery will not make a chair; and I know that it is of about as much value in the physical sciences. Mother Nature is serenely obdurate to honeyed words; only those who understand the ways of things, and can silently and effectually handle them, get any good out of her.

And now ... I will ... tell you what sort of education I should think best adapted for a boy whom one wanted to make a professional anatomist.

I should say, in the first place, let him have a good English elementary education. I do not mean that he shall be able to pass in such and such a standard – that may or may not be an equivalent expression – but that his teaching shall have been such as to have given him command of the common implements of learning and to have created a desire for the things of the understanding.

Further, I should like him to know the elements of physical science, and especially of physics and chemistry, and I should take care that this elementary knowledge was real. I should like my aspirant to be able to read a scientific treatise in Latin, French, or German, because an enormous amount of anatomical knowledge is locked up in those languages. And especially, I should require some ability to draw – I do not mean artistically, for that is a gift which may be cultivated but cannot be learned, but with fair accuracy...

Above all things, let my imaginary pupil have preserved the freshness and vigour of youth in his mind as well as his body. The educational abomination of desolation of the present day is the stimulation of young people to work at high pressure by incessant competitive examinations... The vigour and freshness, which should have been stored up for the purposes of the hard struggle for existence in practical life, have been washed out of them by precocious mental debauchery – by book gluttony and lesson bibbing. Their faculties are worn out by the strain put upon their callow brains, and they are demoralised by worthless childish triumphs before the real work of life begins. I have no compassion for sloth, but youth has more need for intellectual rest than age; and the cheerfulness, the tenacity of purpose, the power of work which make many a successful man what he is, must often be placed to the credit, not of his hours of industry, but to that of his hours of idleness, in boyhood...

This is the sort of education which I should like any one who was going to devote himself to my handicraft to undergo. As to knowing anything about anatomy itself, on the whole I would rather he left that alone until he took it up seriously in my laboratory. It is hard work enough to teach, and I should not like to have superadded to that the possible need of unteaching.

Well, but you will say, this is Hamlet with the Prince of Denmark left out; your 'technical education' is simply a good education, with more attention to physical science, to drawing, and to modern languages than is common, and there is nothing specially technical about it.

Exactly so; that remark takes us straight to the heart of what I have to say; which is, that, in my judgment, the preparatory education of the handicraftsman ought to have nothing of what is ordinarily understood by 'technical' about it.

The workshop is the only real school for a handicraft. The education which precedes that of the workshop should be entirely devoted to the strengthening of the body, the elevation of the moral faculties, and the cultivation of the intelligence; and, especially, to the imbuing the mind with a broad and clear view of the laws of that natural world with the components of which the handicraftsman will have to deal . . .

Now let me apply the lessons I have learned from my handicraft to yours. If any of you were obliged to take an apprentice, I suppose you would like to get a good healthy lad, ready and willing to learn, handy, and with his fingers not all thumbs, as the saying goes. You would like that he should read, write, and cipher well; and, if you were an intelligent master, and your trade involved the application of scientific principles, as so many trades do, you would like him to know enough of the elementary principles of science to understand what was going on. I suppose that, in nine trades out of ten, it would be useful if he could draw; and many of you must have lamented your inability to find out for yourselves what foreigners are doing or have done. So that some knowledge of French and German might, in many cases, be very desirable.

So it appears to me that what you want is pretty much what I want . . . But, on the other hand, if school instruction is carried so far as to encourage bookishness; if the ambition of the scholar is directed, not to the gaining of knowledge, but to the being able to pass examinations successfully; especially if encouragement is given to the mischievous delusion that brainwork is, in itself, and apart from its quality, a nobler or more respectable thing than handi-work – such education may be a deadly mischief to the workman, and lead to the rapid ruin of the industries it is intended to serve . . .

Keeping in mind, then, that the two things to be avoided are, the delay of the entrance of boys into practical life, and the substitution of exhausted bookworms for shrewd, handy men, in our works and factories, let us consider what may be wisely and safely attempted in the way of improving the education of the handicraftsman.

First, I look to the elementary schools now happily established all over the country. I am not going to criticise or find fault with them; on the contrary, their establish-ment seems to me to be the most important and the most beneficial result of the corporate action of the people in our day. A great deal is said of British interests just now, but, depend upon it, that no Eastern difficulty needs our intervention as a nation so seriously, as the putting down both the Bashi-Bazouks of ignorance and the Cossacks of sectarianism at home. What has already been achieved in these directions is a great thing; you must have lived some time to know how great. An education, better in its processes, better in its substance, than that which was accessible to the great majority of well-to-do Britons a quarter of a century ago, is now obtainable by every child in the land. Let any man of my age go into an ordinary elementary school, and unless he was unusually fortunate in his youth, he will tell you that the educational method, the intelligence, patience, and good temper on the teacher's part, which are now at the disposal of the veriest waifs and wastrels of society, are things of which he had no experience in those costly, middle-class schools, which were so ingeniously contrived as to combine all the evils and shortcomings of the great public schools with none of their advantages . . .

But while in view of such an advance in general education, I willingly obey the natural impulse to be thankful, I am not willing altogether to rest. I want to see instruction in elementary science and in art more thoroughly incorporated in the educational system. At present, it is being administered by driblets, as if it were a potent medicine, 'a few drops to be taken occasionally in a teaspoon' . . .

We must seek elsewhere for a supplementary training in these subjects, and, if need be, in foreign languages, which may go on after the workman's life has begun.

The means of acquiring the scientific and artistic part of this training already exists in full working order, in the first place, in the classes of the Science and Art Department, which are, for the most part, held in the evening, so as to be accessible to all who choose to avail themselves of them after working hours . . . All this is, as you may imagine, highly satisfactory to me. I see that spread of scientific education, about which I have so often permitted myself to worry the public, become, for all practical purposes, an accomplished fact . . . Scientific knowledge is spreading by what the alchemists called a 'distillatio per ascensum;' and nothing now can prevent it from continuing to distil upwards and permeate English society, until, in the remote future, there shall be no member of the legislature who does not know as much of science as an elementary school-boy . . .

The great end of life is not knowledge but action. What men need is, as much knowledge as they can assimilate and organise into a basis for action; give them more and it may become injurious. One knows people who are as heavy and stupid from undigested learning as others are from overfulness of meat and drink. But a small percentage of the population is born with that most excellent quality, a desire for excellence, or with special aptitudes of some sort or another . . .

Now the most important object of all educational schemes is to catch these exceptional people, and turn them to account for the good of society. No man can say where they will crop up; like their opposites, the fools and knaves, they appear sometimes in the palace, and sometimes in the hovel; but the great thing to be aimed at, I was almost going to say the most important end of all social arrangements, is to keep these glorious sports of Nature from being either corrupted by luxury or starved by poverty, and to put them into the position in which they can do the work for which they are especially fitted.

Thus, if a lad in an elementary school showed signs of special capacity, I would try to provide him with the means of continuing his education after his daily working life had begun; if in the evening classes he developed special capabilities in the direction of science or of drawing, I would try to secure him an apprenticeship to some trade in which those powers would have applicability. Or, if he chose to become a teacher, he should have the chance of so doing. Finally, to the lad of genius, the one in a million, I would make accessible the highest and most complete training the country could afford. Whatever that might cost, depend upon it the investment would be a good one. I weigh my words when I say that if the nation could purchase a potential Watt, or Davy, or Faraday, at the cost of a hundred thousand pounds down, he would be dirt-cheap at the money . . .

Therefore, as the sum and crown of what is to be done for technical education, I look to the provision of a machinery for winnowing out the capacities and giving them scope. When I was a member of the London School Board, I said, in the course of a speech, that our business was to provide a ladder, reaching from the gutter to the university, along which every child in the three kingdoms should have the chance of climbing as far as he was fit to go. This phrase was so much bandied about at the time, that, to say truth, I am rather tired of it; but I know of no other which so fully expresses my belief, not only about education in general, but about technical education in particular.

The essential foundation of all the organisation needed for the promotion of education among handicraftsmen will, I believe, exist in this country, when every working lad can feel that society has done as much as lies in its power to remove all needless and artificial obstacles from his path; that there is no barrier, except such as exists in the nature of things, between himself and whatever place in the social organisation he is fitted to fill; and, more than this, that, if he has capacity and industry, a hand is held out to help him along any path which is wisely and honestly chosen.

I have endeavoured to point out to you that a great deal of such an organisation already exists; and I am glad to be able to add that there is a good prospect that what is wanting will, before long, be supplemented.

Those powerful and wealthy societies, the livery companies of the City of London, remembering that they are the heirs and representatives of the trade guilds of the Middle Ages, are interesting themselves in the question . . . They have already gone so far as to appoint a committee to act for them; and I betray no confidence in adding that, some time since, the committee sought the advice and assistance of several persons, myself among the number.

Of course I cannot tell you what may be the result of the deliberations of the committee; but we may all fairly hope that, before long, steps which will have a weighty and a lasting influence on the growth and spread of sound and thorough teaching among the handicraftsmen of this country will be taken by the livery companies of London.

Collected Essays, III, 404–26

Address to Working Men's Club and Institute Union, Society of Arts, London, 1 December 1877

Published in *The Fortnightly Review*, XXIX (XXIII n.s.) (1 January 1878), 48

Reprinted in T. H. Huxley, *Science and Culture, and Other Essays* (Macmillan, 1881)

HUME

(1878)

Psychology is a part of the science of life or biology, which differs from the other branches of that science, merely in so far as it deals with the psychical, instead of the physical, phenomena of life.

As there is an anatomy of the body, so there is an anatomy of the mind; the psychologist dissects mental phenomena into elementary states of consciousness as the anatomist resolves limbs into tissues, and tissues into cells ... As the physiologist inquires into the way in which the so-called 'functions' of the body are performed, so the psychologist studies the so-called 'faculties' of the mind. Even a cursory attention to the ways and works of the lower animals suggests a comparative anatomy and physiology of the mind; and the doctrine of evolution presses for application as much in the one field as in the other.

But there is more than a parallel, there is a close and intimate connection between psychology and physiology. No one doubts that, at any rate some mental states are dependent for their existence on the performance of the functions of particular bodily organs. There is no seeing without eyes, and no hearing without ears. If the origin of the contents of the mind is truly a philosophical problem, then the philosopher who attempts to deal with that problem, without acquainting himself with the physiology of sensation, has no more intelligent conception of his business than the physiologist, who thinks he can discuss locomotion without an acquaintance with the principles of mechanics; or respiration, without some tincture of chemistry.

12

On whatever ground we term physiology, science, psychology is entitled to the same appellation; and the method of investigation which elucidates the true relations of the one set of phenomena will discover those of the other. Hence ... it would seem to be an obvious conclusion, that philosophers are likely to be successful in their inquiries, in proportion as they are familiar with the application of scientific method to less abstruse subjects ... And it is accordant with this presumption, that the men who have made the most important positive additions to philosophy, such as Descartes, Spinoza and Kant, not to mention more recent examples, have been deeply imbued with the spirit of physical science; and, in some cases, such as those of Descartes and Kant, have been largely acquainted with its details ... In truth, the laboratory is the fore-court of the temple of philosophy; and whoso has not offered sacrifices and undergone purification there, has little chance of admission into the sanctuary.

Obvious as these considerations may appear to be, it would be wrong to ignore the fact that their force is by no means universally admitted. On the contrary, the necessity for a proper psychological and physiological training to the student of philosophy is denied ... by the 'pure metaphysicians', who attempt to base the theory of knowing upon supposed necessary and universal truths ...

In the language of common life, the 'mind' is spoken of as an entity, independent of the body, though resident in and closely connected with it, and endowed with numerous 'faculties' such as sensibility, understanding, memory, volition, which stand in the same relation to the mind as the organs do to the body, and perform the functions of feeling, reasoning, remembering, and willing ...

The popular classification and terminology of the pheno- mena of consciousness, however, are by no means the first crude conceptions suggested by common sense, but rather a legacy, and, in many respects, a sufficiently *damnosa haereditas*, of ancient philosophy, more or less leavened by theology ... Very little attention to what passes in the mind is sufficient to show, that these conceptions involve assumptions of an extremely hypothetical character. And the first business of the student of psychology is to get rid of such prepossessions; to form conceptions of mental phenomena as they are given us by observation, without any hypothetical admixture, or with only so much as is definitely recognised and held subject to confirmation or otherwise; to classify these phenomena according to their clearly recognisable characters; and to adopt a nomenclature which suggests nothing beyond the results of observation...

According to Locke, 'Knowledge is the perception of the agreement or disagreement of two ideas'; and Hume, though he does not say so in so many words, tacitly accepts the definition. It follows, that neither simple sensation nor simple emotion constitutes knowledge; but that, when impressions of relation are added to these impressions, or their ideas, knowledge arises; and that all knowledge is the knowledge of likenesses and unlikenesses, co-existences and successions.

It really matters very little in what sense terms are used, so long as the same meaning is always rigidly attached to them; and, therefore, it is hardly worth while to quarrel with this generally accepted, though very arbitrary, limitation of the signification of 'knowledge'. But ... the restriction has this unfortunate result, that it excludes all the most intense states of consciousness from any claim to the title of 'knowledge'. For example, on this view, pain, so violent and absorbing as to exclude all other forms of consciousness, is not knowledge; but becomes a part of knowledge the moment we think of it in relation to another pain, or to some other mental phenomenon. Surely this is somewhat inconvenient . . .

But the 'pure metaphysicians' make great capital out of ambiguity. For, starting with the assumption that all knowledge is the perception of relations, and finding themselves like mere common-sense folks, very much disposed to call sensation knowledge, they at once gratify that disposition and save their consistency, by declaring that even the simplest act of sensation contains two terms and a relation – the sensitive subject, the sensigenous object and that masterful entity, the Ego. From which great triad, as from a gnostic Trinity, emanates an endless procession of other logical shadows and all the *Fata Morgana* of philosophical dreamland . . .

Admitting that the sensations, the feelings of pleasure and pain, and those of relation, are the primary irresolvable states of consciousness, two further lines of investigation present themselves. The one leads us to seek the origin of these 'impressions': the other, to inquire into the nature of the steps by which they become metamorphosed into those compound states of consciousness, which so largely enter into our ordinary trains of thought . . .

What we call the operations of the mind are functions of the brain, and the materials of consciousness are products of cerebral activity. Cabanis may have made use of crude and misleading phraseology when he said that the brain secretes thought as the liver secretes bile; but the conception which that much-abused phrase embodies is, nevertheless, far more consistent with fact than the popular notion that the mind is a metaphysical entity . . .

Hume deals with the questions whether all our ideas are derived from experience, or whether, on the contrary, more or fewer of them are innate . . . Whoever denies what is, in fact, an inconceivable proposition, that sensations pass, as such, from the external world into the mind, must admit the conclusion . . . laid down by Descartes, that, strictly speaking, sensations, and *a fortiori*, all the other contents of the mind, are . . . products of the inherent properties of the thinking organ, in which they lie potentially, before they are called into existence by their appropriate causes.

But if all the contents of the mind are innate, what is meant by experience?

It is the conversion, by unknown causes, of these innate potentialities into actual existences. The organ of thought, prior to experience, may be compared to an untouched piano, in which it may be properly said that music is innate, inasmuch as its mechanism contains, potentially, so many octaves of musical notes. The unknown cause of sensation which Descartes calls the 'je ne sais quoi dans les objets', or 'choses telles qu'elles sont', and Kant the 'Noumenon' or 'Ding an sich', is represented by the musician; who, by touching the keys, converts the potentiality of the mechanism into actual sounds. A note so produced is the equivalent of a single experience . . .

If [this] analysis of the phenomena of consciousness . . . is correct, Hume is in error; while the father of modern philosophy had a truer insight, though he overstated the case. For want of sufficiently searching psychological investigations, Descartes was led to suppose that innumerable ideas, the evolution of which in the course of experience can be demonstrated, were direct or innate products of the thinking faculty . . . it is the great merit of Kant that he started afresh on the track indicated by Descartes, and steadily upheld the doctrine of the existence of elements of consciousness, which are neither sense-experiences nor any modifications of them . . .

If . . . all mental states are effects of physical causes, it follows that what are called mental faculties and operations are, properly speaking, cerebral functions, allotted to definite, though not yet precisely assignable, parts of the brain . . . The changes in the nervous matter which bring about the effects which we call its functions, follow upon some kind of stimulus, and rapidly reaching their maximum, as rapidly die away . . . The impulse takes a little time to reach the bell; the bell rings and then becomes quiescent, until another pull is given. . .

If there were a complete likeness between the two terms of this very rough and ready comparison, it is obvious that there could be no such thing as memory. A bell records no audible sign of having been rung five minutes ago, and the activity of a sensigenous cerebral particle might similarly leave no trace . . . But the special peculiarity of the cerebral apparatus is, that any given function which has once been performed is very easily set a-going again, by causes more or less different from those to which it owed its origin. Of the mechanism of this generation of images of impressions or ideas (in Hume's sense), which may be termed *Ideation*, we know nothing at present, though the fact and its results are familiar enough . . .

The rapidity and the intensity of this ideational process are obviously dependent upon physiological conditions. The widest differences in these respects are constitutional in men of different temperaments; and are observable in oneself, under varying conditions of hunger and repletion, fatigue and freshness, calmness and emotional excitement . . . No great attention to what passes in the mind is needful to prove that our trains of thought are neither to be arrested, nor even permanently controlled, by our desires or emotions. Nevertheless they are largely influenced by them. In the presence of a strong desire, or emotion, the stream of thought no longer flows on in a straight course, but seems, as it were, to eddy round the idea of that which is the object of emotion . . . And as, on the one hand, it is so hard to drive away the thought we would fain be rid of; so, upon the other, the pleasant imaginations which we would so gladly retain are, sooner or later, jostled away by the crowd of claimants for birth into the world of consciousness; which hover ... in the limbo of the brain ...

It is a curious omission on Hume's part that while ... dwelling on two classes of ideas, *Memories* and *Imaginations*, he has not, at the same time, taken notice of a third group ... *Expectations;* which differ from simple imaginations in being associated with the idea of the existence of corresponding impressions in the future, just as memories contain the idea of the existence of the corresponding impressions in the past ...

When complex impressions or complex ideas are reproduced as memories, it is probable that the copies never give all the details of the originals with perfect accuracy, and it is certain that they rarely do so ... Almost all, if not all, our memories are therefore sketches, rather than portraits, of the originals – the salient features are obvious, while the subordinate characters are obscure or unrepresented ...

The generic ideas which are formed from several similar, but not identical, complex experiences are what are commonly called *abstract* or *general* ideas; and Berkeley endeavoured to prove that all general ideas are nothing but particular ideas annexed to a certain term, which gives them a more extensive signification, and makes them recall, upon occasion, other individuals which are similar to them ... Berkeley's view appears to be largely applicable to such general ideas as are formed after language has been acquired, and to all the more abstract sort of conceptions, [but] general ideas ... may exist independently of language ...

An anatomist who occupies himself intently with the examination of several specimens of some new kind of animal, in course of time acquires so vivid a conception of its form and structure, that the idea may take visible shape and become a sort of waking dream. But the figure which thus presents itself is generic, not specific. It is no copy of any one specimen, but, more or less, a mean of the series; and there seems no reason to doubt that the minds of children before they learn to speak, and of deaf mutes, are peopled with similarly generated generic ideas of sensible objects . . . It is hardly to be doubted that children have very distinct memories long before they can speak; and . . . they act upon their memories . . . they to all intents and purposes believe their memories. In other words, though, being devoid of language, the child cannot frame a proposition expressive of belief; cannot say 'sugar-plum was sweet'; yet the psychical operation of which that proposition is merely the verbal expression, is perfectly effected . . .

The reasoning which applied to memories applies to expectations. To have an expectation of a given event, and to believe that it will happen, are only two modes of stating the same fact. Again, just in the same way as we call a memory, put into words, a belief, so we give the same name to an expectation in like clothing. And the fact already cited, that a child before it can speak acts upon its memories, is good evidence that it forms expectations . . . Thus, beliefs of expectations, or at any rate their potentialities, are, as much of those of memory, antecedent to speech, and are as incapable of justification by any logical process . . .

Hume has attached somewhat too exclusive a weight to . . . repetition of experiences . . . and any one who will make the experiment will find, that one burning is quite sufficient to establish an indissoluble belief that contact with fire and pain go together . . . Hence, while a belief of expectation is, in most cases . . . established by custom, or the repetition of weak impressions, it may quite well be based upon a single strong experience...

But, that which is, under the one aspect, the strengthening of a memory, is, under the other, the intensification of an expectation ... And it is important to note that such expectations may be formed quite unconsciously. In my dressing-room, a certain can is usually kept full of water, and I am in the habit of lifting it to pour out water for washing. Sometimes the servant has forgotten to fill it, and then I find that, when I take hold of the handle, the can goes up with a jerk. Long association has, in fact, led me to expect the can to have a considerable weight; and, quite unawares, my muscular effort is adjusted to the expectation.

The process of strengthening generic memories of succession, and, at the same time, intensifying expectations of succession, is what is commonly called *verification*. The impression B had frequently been observed to follow the impression A ... And repeated verification may render that expectation so strong that its non-verification is inconceivable...

If any weight is to be attached to arguments from analogy, there is overwhelming evidence in favour of the belief that children, before they can speak, and deaf mutes, possess the feelings to which those who have acquired the faculty of speech apply the name of sensations; that they have the feelings of relation; that trains of ideas pass through their minds; that generic ideas are formed from specific ones; and, that among these, ideas of memory and expectation occupy a most important place, inasmuch as, in their quality of potential beliefs, they furnish the grounds of action ...

But ... whatever cogency is attached to the arguments in favour of the occurrence of all the fundamental phenomena of mind in young children and deaf mutes, an equal force must be allowed to appertain to those which may be adduced to prove that the higher animals have minds . . . It is not merely that the observation of the actions of animals almost irresistibly suggests the attribution to them of mental states, such as those which accompany corresponding actions in men. The minute comparison which has been instituted by anatomists and physiologists between the organs which we know to constitute the apparatus of thought in man, and the corresponding organs in brutes, has demonstrated the existence of the closest similarity between the two, not only in structure, as far as the microscope will carry us, but in function, as far as functions are determinable by experiment . . . And the suggestion that we must stop at the exact point at which direct proof fails us; and refuse to believe that the similarity which extends so far stretches yet further, is no better than a quibble. Robinson Crusoe did not feel bound to conclude, from the single human footprint which he saw in the sand, that the maker of the impression had only one leg . . .

In short, it seems hard to assign any good reason for denying to the higher animals any mental state, or process, in which the employment of the vocal or visual symbols of which language is composed is not involved . . . [However,] in those forms of animal life in which the nervous apparatus has reached no higher degree of development, than that exhibited by the system of the spinal cord and the foundation of the brain in ourselves, the argument from analogy leaves the assumption of the existence of any form of consciousness unsupported . . .

The process of argument, or reasoning in man is based upon potential beliefs of expectation, which are formed in the man exactly in the same way as in the animal. But, in men endowed with speech, the mental state which constitutes the potential belief is represented by a verbal proposition . . . [which] has come to be regarded as a reality, instead of as the mere symbol which it really is; and that reasoning, or logic, which deals with nothing but propositions, is supposed to be necessary in order to validate the natural fact symbolised by those propositions. It is a fallacy similar to that of supposing that money is the foundation of wealth, whereas it is only the wholly unessential symbol of property . . .

Hume's views respecting necessary truths, and more particularly concerning causation, have, more than any other part of his teaching, contributed to give him a prominent place in the history of philosophy . . . much stress has been laid upon Hume's admission that the truths of mathematics are intuitively and demonstratively certain; in other words, that they are necessary and, in that respect, differ from all other kinds of belief . . . [But] Suppose that there were no such things as impressions of sight and touch anywhere in the universe, what idea could we have even of a straight line, much less of a triangle and of the relations between its sides? . . . unless a man had seen or felt the difference between a straight line and a crooked one, straight and crooked would have no more meaning to him than red and blue to the blind . . .

Whatever may be the differences between mathematical and other truths, they do not justify Hume's statement. And . . . if the axioms of mathematics are innate, nature would seem to have taken unnecessary trouble; since the ordinary process of association appears to be amply sufficient to confer upon them all the universality and necessity which they actually possess . . .

It is commonly urged that the axiom of causation cannot be derived from experience, because experience only proves that many things have causes, whereas the axiom declares that all things have causes. The syllogism, 'many things which come into existence have causes. A has come into existence: therefore A had a cause', is obviously fallacious, if A is not previously shown to be one of the 'many things'. And this objection is perfectly sound so far as it goes. The axiom of causation cannot possibly be deduced from any general proposition which simply embodies experience. But it does not follow that the belief, or expectation, expressed by the axiom, is not a product of experience, generated antecedently to, and altogether independently of, the logically unjustifiable language in which we express it.

In fact, the axiom of causation resembles all other beliefs of expectation in being the verbal symbol of a purely automatic act of the mind, which is altogether extra-logical, and would be illogical, if it were not constantly verified by experience. Experience, as we have seen, stores up memories; memories generate expectations or beliefs ...But to seek for the reason of the facts in the verbal symbols by which they are expressed, and to be astonished that it is not to be found there, is surely singular...

Whatever it is that leads us to seek for a cause for every event, in the case of the phenomena of the external world, compels us, with equal cogency, to seek it in that of the mind.

The only meaning of the law of causation, in the physical world, is, that it generalises universal experience of the order of that world; and, if experience shows a similar order to obtain among states of consciousness, the law of causation will properly express that order...

The last asylum of the hard-pressed advocate of the doctrine of uncaused volition is usually, that, argue as you like, he has a profound and ineradicable consciousness of what he calls the freedom of his will. But ... the moment the attempt is made to give a definite meaning to the words, the supposed opposition between free will and necessity turns out to be a mere verbal dispute.

Half the controversies about the freedom of the will...
rest upon the absurd presumption that the proposition,
'I can do as I like', is contradictory to the doctrine of
necessity. The answer is: nobody doubts that, at any rate
within certain limits, you can do as you like. But what
determines your likings and dislikings? ... The passionate
assertion of the consciousness of their freedom, which is
the favourite refuge of the opponents of the doctrine of
necessity, is mere futility, for nobody denies it. What they
really have to do, if they would upset the necessarian
argument, is to prove ... that, whatever may be the
fixity of order of the universe of things, that of thought is
given over to chance...

A person is held responsible only for those acts which
are preceded by a certain intention; and, as we cannot see,
or hear, or feel, an intention, we can only reason out its
existence on the principle that like effects have like causes.

If a man is found by the police busy with 'jemmy' and
dark lantern at a jeweller's shop door over night, the
magistrate before whom he is brought the next morning,
reasons from those effects to their causes in the fellow's
burglarious ideas and volitions, with perfect confidence,
and punishes him accordingly ... A man's moral responsibility for his acts has, in fact, nothing to do with the
causation of these acts, but depends on the frame of mind
which accompanies them...

So far, therefore, from necessity destroying moral
responsibility, it is the foundation of all praise and blame;
and moral admiration reaches its climax in the ascription of
necessary goodness to the Deity...

Whether the public like to be deceived, or not, may be
open to question; but it is beyond a doubt that they love to
be shocked in a pleasant and mannerly way. Now Hume's
speculations on moral questions ... support the cause of

righteousness in a cool, reasonable, indeed slightly patronising fashion, eminently in harmony with the mind of the eighteenth century; which admired virtue very much, if she would only avoid the rigour which the age called fanaticism, and the fervour which it called enthusiasm . . .

No qualities give a man a greater claim to personal merit than benevolence and justice; but if we inquire why benevolence deserves so much praise, the answer will certainly contain a large reference to the utility of that virtue to society; and as for justice, the very existence of the virtue implies that of society . . . But granting the utility to society of all kinds of benevolence and justice, why should the quality of those virtues involve the sense of moral obligation? . . .

The feeling of obligation to be just, or of the duty of justice, arises out of that association of moral approbation or disapprobation with one's own actions, which is what we call conscience. To fail in justice, or in benevolence, is to be displeased with one's self. But happiness is impossible without inward self-approval; and, hence, every man who has any regard to his own happiness and welfare, will find his best reward in the practice of every moral duty. On this topic Hume expends much eloquence . . .

In [Hume's] paean to virtue, there is more of the dance measure than will sound appropriate in the ears of most of the pilgrims who toil painfully, not without many a stumble and many a bruise, along the rough and steep roads which lead to the higher life . . . The calculation of the greatest happiness is not performed quite so easily as a rule of three sum; while, in the hour of temptation, the question will crop up, whether, as something has to be sacrificed, a bird in the hand is not worth two in the bush; whether it may not be as well to give up the problematical greater happiness in the future, for a certain great happiness in the present . . .

In whichever way we look at the matter, morality is

based on feeling, not on reason, though reason alone is competent to trace out the effects of our actions and thereby dictate conduct. Justice is founded on the love of one's neighbour; and goodness is a kind of beauty. The moral law, like the laws of physical nature, rests in the long run upon instinctive intuitions, and is neither more nor less 'innate' and 'necessary' than they are. Some people cannot by any means be got to understand the first book of Euclid; but the truths of mathematics are no less necessary and binding on the great mass of mankind. Some there are who cannot feel the difference between the 'Sonata Appassionata' and 'Cherry Ripe'; or between a grave-stone-cutter's cherub and the Apollo Belvidere; but the canons of art are none the less acknowledged. While some there may be, who, devoid of sympathy, are incapable of a sense of duty; but neither does their existence affect the foundations of morality. Such pathological deviations from true manhood are merely the halt, the lame, and the blind of the world of consciousness; and the anatomist of the mind leaves them aside, as the anatomist of the body would ignore abnormal specimens.

And as there are Pascals and Mozarts, Newtons and Raffaelles, in whom the innate faculty for science or art seems to need but a touch to spring into full vigour: and through whom the human race obtains new possibilities of knowledge and new conceptions of beauty; so there have been men of moral genius, to whom we owe ideals of duty and visions of moral perfection, which ordinary mankind could never have attained: though, happily for them, they can feel the beauty of a vision, which lay beyond the reach of their dull imaginations, and count life well spent in shaping some faint image of it in the actual world...

Collected Essays, VI, 3–240
Published as T. H. Huxley, *Hume* (Macmillan, 1878)

SCIENCE AND CULTURE

(1880)

Six years ago, as some of my present hearers may remember, I had the privilege of addressing a large assemblage of the inhabitants of this city [Birmingham], who had gathered together to do honour to the memory of their famous townsman, Joseph Priestley, [and] ... celebrated the centenary of his chief discovery ... For us children of the nineteenth century, however, the establishment of a college under the conditions of Sir Josiah Mason's Trust, has a significance apart from any which it could have possessed a hundred years ago ...

From the time that the first suggestion to introduce physical science into ordinary education was timidly whispered, until now, the advocates of scientific education have met with opposition of two kinds. On the one hand, they have been pooh-poohed by the men of business who pride themselves on being the representatives of practicality; while, on the other hand, they have been excommunicated by the classical scholars, in their capacity of Levites in charge of the ark of culture ...

Sir Josiah Mason, without doubt most wisely, has left very large freedom of action to the trustees ... But, with respect to three points, he has laid most explicit injunctions upon both administrators and teachers.

Party politics are forbidden to enter into the minds of either, so far as the work of the College is concerned; theology is as sternly banished from its precincts; and finally, it is especially declared that the College shall make no provision for 'mere literary instruction and education'.

It does not concern me at present to dwell upon the first two injunctions any longer than may be needful to express my full conviction of their wisdom. But the third prohibition brings us face to face with those other opponents of scientific education, who are by no means in the moribund condition of the practical man, but alive, alert, and formidable . . .

How often have we not been told that the study of physical [natural] science is incompetent to confer culture; that it touches none of the higher problems of life; and, what is worse, that the continual devotion to scientific studies tends to generate a narrow and bigoted belief in the applicability of scientific methods to the search after truth of all kinds? How frequently one has reason to observe that no reply to a troublesome argument tells so well as calling its author a 'mere scientific specialist'. And, as I am afraid it is not permissible to speak of this form of opposition to scientific education in the past tense; may we not expect to be told that this, not only omission, but prohibition, of 'mere literary instruction and education' is a patent example of scientific narrow-mindedness?

I am not acquainted with Sir Josiah Mason's reasons for the action which he has taken; but if, as I apprehend is the case, he refers to the ordinary classical course of our schools and universities by the name of 'mere literary instruction and education', I venture to offer sundry reasons of my own in support of that action.

For I hold very strongly by two convictions – The first is, that neither the discipline nor the subject-matter of classical education is of such direct value to the student of physical science as to justify the expenditure of valuable time upon either; and the second is, that for the purpose of attaining real culture, an exclusively scientific education is at least as effectual as an exclusively literary education.

13

I need hardly point out to you that these opinions, especially the latter, are diametrically opposed to those of the great majority of educated Englishmen, influenced as they are by school and university traditions. In their belief, culture is obtainable only by a liberal education; and a liberal education is synonymous, not merely with education and instruction in literature, but in one particular form of literature, namely, that of Greek and Roman antiquity. They hold that the man who has learned Latin and Greek, however little, is educated; while he who is versed in other branches of knowledge, however deeply, is a more or less respectable specialist, not admissible into the cultural caste. The stamp of the educated man, the University degree, is not for him.

I am too well acquainted with the generous catholicity of spirit, the true sympathy with scientific thought, which pervades the writings of our chief apostle of culture [Matthew Arnold] to identify him with these opinions; and yet one may cull from one and another of those epistles to the Philistines, which so much delight all who do not answer to that name, sentences which lend them some support.

Mr. Arnold tells us that the meaning of culture is 'to know the best that has been thought and said in the world'. It is the criticism of life contained in literature ... We have here to deal with two distinct propositions. The first, that a criticism of life is the essence of culture; the second, that literature contains the materials which suffice for the construction of such a criticism.

I think that we must all assent to the first proposition. For culture certainly means something quite different from learning or technical skill. It implies the possession of an ideal, and the habit of critically estimating the value of things by comparison with a theoretic standard. Perfect culture should supply a complete theory of life, based upon a clear knowledge alike of its possibilities and of its limitations.

But we may agree to all this, and yet strongly dissent from the assumption that literature alone is competent to supply this knowledge. . . . Indeed, to any one acquainted with the scope of physical science, it is not at all evident . . . I should say that an army, without weapons of precision and with no particular base of operations, might more hopefully enter upon a campaign on the Rhine, than a man devoid of knowledge of what physical science has done in the last century, upon a criticism of life . . .

The business of the philosophers of the middle ages was to deduce from the data furnished by the theologians, conclusions in accordance with ecclesiastical decrees. They were allowed the high privilege of showing, by logical process, how and why that which the Church said was true, must be true. And if their demonstrations fell short of or exceeded this limit, the Church was maternally ready to check their aberrations; if need were by the help of the secular arm.

Between the two, our ancestors were furnished with a compact and complete criticism of life. They were told how the world began and how it would end; they learned that all material existence was but a base and insignificant blot upon the face of the spiritual world, and that nature was, to all intents and purposes, the play-ground of the devil; they learned that the earth is the centre of the visible universe, and that man is the cynosure of things terrestrial; and more especially was it inculcated that the course of nature had no fixed order, but that it could be, and constantly was, altered by the agency of innumerable spiritual beings, good and bad, according as they were moved by the deeds and prayers of men. The sum and substance of the whole doctrine was to produce the conviction that the only thing really worth knowing in this world was how to secure that place in a better which, under certain conditions, the Church promised . . .

Had the western world been left to itself in Chinese isolation, there is no saying how long this state of things might have endured. But, happily, it was not left to itself. Even earlier than the thirteenth century, the development of Moorish civilisation in Spain and the great movement of the Crusades had introduced the leaven which, from that day to this, has never ceased to work. At first, through the intermediation of Arabic translations, afterwards by the study of the originals, the western nations of Europe became acquainted with the writings of the ancient philosophers and poets, and, in time, with the whole of the vast literature of antiquity . . . Those who possessed it prided themselves on having attained the highest culture then within the reach of mankind.

And justly. For saving Dante on his solitary pinnacle, there was no figure in modern literature at the time of the Renascence to compare with the men of antiquity; there was no art to compete with their sculpture; there was no physical science but that which Greece had created. Above all, there was no other example of perfect intellectual freedom – of the unhesitating acceptance of reason as the sole guide to truth and the supreme arbiter of conduct.

The new learning necessarily soon exerted a profound influence upon education. The language of the monks and schoolmen seemed little better than gibberish to scholars fresh from Virgil and Cicero, and the study of Latin was placed upon a new foundation. Moreover, Latin itself ceased to afford the sole key to knowledge. The student who sought the highest thought of antiquity, found only a second-hand reflection of it in Roman literature, and turned his face to the full light of the Greeks. And after a battle, not altogether dissimilar to that which is at present being fought over the teaching of physical science, the study of Greek was recognised as an essential element of all higher education.

Thus the Humanists, as they were called, won the day; and the great reform which they effected was of incalculable service to mankind. But the Nemesis of all reformers is finality; and the reformers of education, like those of religion, fell into the profound, however common, error of mistaking the beginning for the end of the work of reformation.

The representatives of the Humanists, in the nineteenth century, take their stand upon classical education as the sole avenue to culture, as firmly as if we were still in the age of Renascence. Yet, surely, the present intellectual relations of the modern and ancient worlds are profoundly different from those which obtained three centuries ago. Leaving aside the existence of a great and characteristically modern literature, of modern painting, and, especially, of modern music, there is one feature of the present state of the civilised world which separates it more widely from the Renascence, than the Renascence was separated from the middle ages.

This distinctive character of our own times lies in the vast and constantly increasing part which is played by natural knowledge. Not only is our daily life shaped by it, not only does the prosperity of millions of men depend upon it, but our whole theory of life has long been influenced, consciously or unconsciously, by the general conceptions of the universe, which have been forced upon us by physical science . . .

There is no great force in the *tu quoque* argument, or else the advocates of scientific education might fairly enough retort upon the modern Humanists that they may be learned specialists, but that they possess no such sound foundation for a criticism of life as deserves the name of culture. And, indeed, if we were disposed to be cruel, we might urge that the Humanists have brought this reproach upon themselves, not because they are too full of the spirit of the ancient Greek, but because they lack it.

The period of the Renascence is commonly called that of the 'Revival of Letters', as if the influences then brought to bear upon the mind of Western Europe had been wholly exhausted in the field of literature. I think it is very commonly forgotten that the revival of science, effected by the same agency, although less conspicuous, was not less momentous.

In fact, the few and scattered students of nature of that day picked up the clue to her secrets exactly as it fell from the hands of the Greeks a thousand years before. The foundations of mathematics were so well laid by them, that our children learn their geometry from a book written for the schools of Alexandria two thousand years ago. Modern astronomy is the natural continuation and development of the work of Hipparchus and of Ptolemy; modern physics of that of Democritus and of Archimedes; it was long before modern biological science outgrew the knowledge bequeathed to us by Aristotle, by Theophrastus, and by Galen.

We cannot know all the best thoughts and sayings of the Greeks unless we know what they thought about natural phaenomena. We cannot fully apprehend their criticism of life unless we understand the extent to which that criticism was affected by scientific conceptions. We falsely pretend to be the inheritors of their culture, unless we are penetrated, as the best minds among them were, with an unhesitating faith that the free employment of reason, in accordance with scientific method, is the sole method of reaching truth . . .

Nevertheless, I am the last person to question the importance of genuine literary education, or to suppose that intellectual culture can be complete without it. An exclusively scientific training will bring about a mental twist as surely as an exclusively literary training. The value of the cargo does not compensate for a ship's being out of trim; and I should be very sorry to think that the Scientific College would turn out none but lop-sided men.

There is no need, however, that such a catastrophe should happen. Instruction in English, French, and German is provided, and thus the three greatest literatures of the modern world are made accessible to the student . . . But even supposing that the knowledge of [foreign] languages acquired is not more than sufficient for purely scientific purposes, every Englishman has, in his native tongue, an almost perfect instrument of literary expression; and, in his own literature, models of every kind of literary excellence. If an Englishman cannot get literary culture out of his Bible, his Shakespeare, his Milton, neither, in my belief, will the profoundest study of Homer and Sophocles, Virgil and Horace, give it to him.

Thus, since . . . artistic instruction is also contemplated, it seems to me that a fairly complete culture is offered to all who are willing to take advantage of it . . .

I confess, I should like to see one addition made to the excellent scheme of education propounded for the College, in the shape of provision for the teaching of Sociology. For though we are all agreed that party politics are to have no place in the instruction of the College; yet in this country, practically governed as it is now by universal suffrage, every man who does his duty must exercise political functions. And, if the evils which are inseparable from the good of political liberty are to be checked, if the perpetual oscillation of nations between anarchy and despotism is to be replaced by the steady march of self-restraining freedom; it will be because men will gradually bring themselves to deal with political, as they now deal with scientific questions; to be as ashamed of undue haste and partisan prejudice in the one case as in the other; and to believe that the machinery of society is at least as delicate as that of a spinning-jenny, and as little likely to be improved by the meddling of those who have not taken the trouble to master the principles of its action...

Collected Essays, III, 134–59

Address at opening of Mason College, Birmingham, 1 October 1880

Published in T. H. Huxley, *Science and Culture, and Other Essays* (Macmillan, 1881)

ON SCIENCE AND ART
IN RELATION TO EDUCATION
(1883)

Some fourteen years ago I was the guest of a citizen of
yours ... at a very charming and pleasant dinner given by
the Philomathic Society; and I there and then, and in this
very city [Liverpool], made a speech upon the topic of
Scientific Education...

Now, the points to which I directed particular attention
on that occasion were these: in the first place, that instruction in physical [natural] science supplies information of a
character of especial value, both in a practical and a speculative point of view – information which cannot be obtained
otherwise; and, in the second place, that, as educational
discipline, it supplies, in a better form than any other
study can supply, exercise in a special form of logic, and a
peculiar method of testing the validity of our processes of
inquiry. I said further, that, even at that time, a great and
increasing attention was being paid to physical science in
our schools and colleges, and that, most assuredly, such
attention must go on growing and increasing, until education in these matters occupied a very much larger share of
the time which is given to teaching and training, than had
been the case heretofore...

How far does the experience of the last fourteen years
justify the estimate which I ventured to put forward of the
value of scientific culture, and of the share – the increasing
share – which it must take in ordinary education?...

I remember, some few years ago, hearing of the head-
master of a large school, who had expressed great dis-
satisfaction with the adoption of the teaching of physical

science – and that after experiment. But the experiment consisted in this – in asking one of the junior masters in the school to get up science, in order to teach it; and the young gentleman went away for a year and got up science and taught it. Well, I have no doubt that the result was as disappointing as the head-master said it was, and I have no doubt that it ought to have been as disappointing, and far more disappointing too; for, if this kind of instruction is to be of any good at all, if it is not to be less than no good, if it is to take the place of that which is already of some good, then there are several points which must be attended to.

And the first of these is the proper selection of topics, the second is practical teaching, the third is practical teachers, and the fourth is sufficiency of time. If these four points are not carefully attended to by anybody who undertakes the teaching of physical science in schools, my advice to him is to let it alone. I will not dwell at any length upon the first point, because there is a general consensus of opinion as to the nature of the topics which should be chosen. The second point – practical teaching – is one of great importance, because it requires more capital to set it agoing, demands more time, and, last, but by no means least, it requires much more personal exertion and trouble on the part of those professing to teach than is the case with other kinds of instruction...

I remember, in my youth, there were detestable books which ought to have been burned by the hands of the common hangman, for they contained questions and answers to be learned by heart, of this sort, 'What is a horse? The horse is termed *Equus caballus;* belongs to the class Mammalia; order, Pachydermata; family, Solidungula.' Was any human being wiser for learning that magic formula? Was he not more foolish, inasmuch as he was deluded into taking words for knowledge? It is that kind of teaching that one wants to get rid of, and banished out of science. Make it as little as you like, but, unless that which is taught is based on actual observation and familiarity with facts, it is better left alone.

There are a great many people who imagine that elementary teaching might be properly carried out by teachers provided with only elementary knowledge. Let me assure you that that is the profoundest mistake in the world. There is nothing so difficult to do as to write a good elementary book, and there is nobody so hard to teach properly and well as people who know nothing about a subject, and I will tell you why. If I address an audience of persons who are occupied in the same line of work as myself, I can assume that they know a vast deal, and that they can find out the blunders I make. If they don't, it is their fault and not mine; but when I appear before a body of people who know nothing about the matter, who take for gospel whatever I say, surely it becomes needful that I consider what I say, make sure that it will bear examination, and that I do not impose upon the credulity of those who have faith in me. In the second place, it involves that difficult process of knowing what you know so well that you can talk about it as you can talk about your ordinary business. A man can always talk about his own business. He can always make it plain; but, if his knowledge is hearsay, he is afraid to go beyond what he has recollected, and put it before those that are ignorant in such a shape that they shall comprehend it. That is why, to be a good elementary teacher, to teach the elements of any subject, requires most careful consideration, if you are a master of the subject; and, if you are not a master of it, it is needful you should familiarise yourself with so much as you are called upon to teach – soak yourself in it, so to speak – until you know it as part of your daily life and daily knowledge, and then you will be able to teach anybody . . .

The last point I have referred to is the question of the sufficiency of time. And here comes the rub. The teaching of science needs time, as any other subject; but it needs more time proportionally than other subjects, for the amount of work obviously done, if the teaching is to be, as I have said, practical. Work done in a laboratory involves a good deal of expenditure of time without always an obvious result, because we do not see anything of that quiet process of soaking the facts into the mind, which takes place through the organs of the senses. On this ground there must be ample time given to science teaching. What that amount of time should be . . . is a point which cannot be settled until one has made up one's mind about various other questions . . .

I know quite well that launching myself into this discussion is a very dangerous operation . . . But the discussion is so fundamental . . . that I will even venture to make the experiment . . . Next to being right in this world, the best of all things is to be clearly and definitely wrong, because you will come out somewhere. If you go buzzing about between right and wrong, vibrating and fluctuating, you come out nowhere; but if you are absolutely and thoroughly and persistently wrong, you must, some of these days, have the extreme good fortune of knocking your head against a fact, and that sets you all straight again. So I will not trouble myself as to whether I may be right or wrong in what I am about to say, but at any rate I hope to be clear and definite; and then you will be able to judge for yourselves whether, in following out the train of thought I have to introduce, you knock your heads against facts or not . . .

Now, it is a very remarkable fact – but it is true of most things in this world – that there is hardly anything one-sided, or of one nature; and it is not immediately obvious what of the things that interest us may be regarded as pure science, and what may be regarded as pure art . . . Taking the generality of mankind, I think it may be said that, when they begin to learn mathematics, their whole souls are absorbed in tracing the connection between the premises and the conclusion, and that to them geometry is pure science. So I think it may be said that mechanics and osteology are pure science. On the other hand, melody in music is pure art. You cannot reason about it; there is no proposition involved in it. So, again, in the pictorial art, an arabesque, or a 'harmony in grey', touches none but the aesthetic faculty. But a great mathematician, and even many persons who are not great mathematicians, will tell you that they derive immense pleasure from geometrical reasonings. Everybody knows mathematicians speak of solutions and problems as 'elegant', and they tell you that a certain mass of mystic symbols is 'beautiful, quite lovely'. Well, you do not see it. They do see it, because the intellectual process, the process of comprehending the reasons symbolised by these figures and these signs, confers upon them a sort of pleasure, such as an artist has in visual symmetry. Take a science of which I may speak with more confidence, and which is the most attractive of those I am concerned with. It is what we call morphology, which consists in tracing out the unity in variety of the infinitely diversified structures of animals and plants. I cannot give you any example of a thorough aesthetic pleasure more intensely real than a pleasure of this kind – the pleasure which arises in one's mind when a whole mass of different structures run into one harmony as the expression of a central law. That is where the province of art overlays and embraces the province of intellect. And, if I may venture to express an opinion on such a subject, the great majority of forms of art are not in the sense what I just now defined them to be – pure art; but they derive much of their quality from simultaneous and even unconscious excitement of the intellect.

When I was a boy, I was very fond of music, and I am so now; and it so happened that I had the opportunity of hearing much good music . . . I remember perfectly well – though I knew nothing about music then, and, I may add, know nothing whatever about it now – the intense satisfaction and delight which I had in listening, by the hour together, to Bach's fugues. It is a pleasure which remains with me, I am glad to think; but, of late years, I have tried to find out why and wherefore, and it has often occurred to me that the pleasure derived from musical compositions of this kind is essentially of the same nature as that which is derived from pursuits which are commonly regarded as purely intellectual. I mean, that the source of pleasure is exactly the same as in most of my problems in morphology – that you have the theme in one of the old master's works followed out in all its endless variations, always appearing and always reminding you of unity in variety . . .

If we turn to literature, the same thing is true, and you find works of literature which may be said to be pure art. A little song of Shakespeare or of Goethe is pure art; it is exquisitely beautiful, although its intellectual content may be nothing. A series of pictures is made to pass before your mind by the meaning of words, and the effect is a melody of ideas. Nevertheless, the great mass of the literature we esteem is valued, not merely because of having artistic form, but because of its intellectual content; and the value is the higher the more precise, distinct, and true is that intellectual content. And if you will let me for a moment speak of the very highest forms of literature, do we not regard them as highest simply because the more we know the truer they seem, and the more competent we are to appreciate beauty the more beautiful they are ? No man ever understands Shakespeare until he is old, though the youngest may admire him, the reason being that he satisfies the artistic instinct of the youngest and harmonises with the ripest and richest experience of the oldest.

I have said this much to draw your attention to what, in my mind, lies at the root of all this matter, and at the understanding of one another by the men of science on the one hand, and the men of literature, and history, and art, on the other. It is not a question whether one order of study or another should predominate. It is a question of what topics of education you shall select which will combine all the needful elements in such due proportion as to give the greatest amount of food, support, and encouragement, to those faculties which enable us to appreciate truth, and to profit by those sources of innocent happiness which are open to us, and, at the same time, to avoid that which is bad, and coarse, and ugly, and keep clear of the multitude of pitfalls and dangers which beset those who break through the natural or moral laws.

I address myself, in this spirit, to the consideration of the question of the value of purely literary education. Is it good and sufficient, or is it insufficient and bad? Well, here I venture to say that there are literary educations and literary educations. If I am to understand by that term ... keeping boys for eight or ten years at learning the rules of Latin and Greek grammar, construing certain Latin and Greek authors, and possibly making verses which, had they been English verses, would have been condemned as abominable doggerel – if that is what you mean by literary education, then I say it is scandalously insufficient and almost worthless ... I say the thing professes to be literary education that is not a literary education at all. It was not literature at all that was taught, but science in a very bad form ... The analysis of a text by the help of the rules of grammar is just as much a scientific operation as the analysis of a chemical compound by the help of the rules of chemical analysis. There is nothing that appeals to the aesthetic faculty in that operation ... Then you may say, 'If that is so, if the education was scientific, why cannot you be satisfied with it?' I say, because although it is a scientific training, it is of the most inadequate and inappropriate kind...

I desire to speak with the utmost respect of that science – philology – of which grammar is a part and parcel; yet everybody knows that grammar, as it is usually learned at school, affords no scientific training. It is taught just as you would teach the rules of chess or draughts. On the other hand, if I am to understand by a literary education the study of the literatures of either ancient or modern nations – but especially those of antiquity, and especially that of ancient Greece; if this literature is studied, not merely from the point of view of philological science, and its practical application to the interpretation of texts, but as an exemplification of and commentary upon the principles of art; if you look upon the literature of a people as a chapter in the development of the human mind, if you work out this in a broad spirit, and with such collateral references to morals and politics, and physical geography, and the like as are needful to make you comprehend what the meaning of ancient literature and civilisation is – then, assuredly, it affords a splendid and noble education. But I still think it is susceptible of improvement, and that no man will ever comprehend the real secret of the difference between the ancient world and our present time, unless he has learned to see the difference which the late development of physical science has made between the thought of this day and the thought of that...

Among scientific topics, using the word scientific in the broadest sense, I would also include the elements of the theory of morals and of that of political and social life, which, strangely enough, it never seems to occur to anybody to teach a child. I would have the history of our own country, and of all the influences which have been brought to bear upon it, with incidental geography, not as a mere chronicle of reigns and battles, but as a chapter in the development of the race, and the history of civilisation.

Then with respect to aesthetic knowledge and discipline, we have happily in the English language one of the most magnificent storehouses of artistic beauty and of models of literary excellence which exists in the world at the present time ... and I would assuredly devote a very large portion of the time of every English child to the careful study of the models of English writing of such varied and wonderful kind as we possess, and, what is still more important and still more neglected, the habit of using that language with precision, with force, and with art. I fancy we are almost the only nation in the world who seem to think that composition comes by nature. The French attend to their own language, the Germans study theirs; but Englishmen do not seem to think it is worth their while. Nor would I fail to include, in the course of study I am sketching, translations of all the best works of antiquity, or of the modern world ... You won't get all you would get from the original, but you may get a great deal; and to refuse to know this great deal because you cannot get all, seems to be as sensible as for a hungry man to refuse bread because he cannot get partridge. Finally, I would add instruction in either music or painting, or, if the child should be so unhappy, as sometimes happens, as to have no faculty for either of those, and no possibility of doing anything in any artistic sense with them, then I would see what could be done with literature alone; but I would provide, in the fullest sense, for the development of the aesthetic side of the mind. In my judgment, those are all the essentials of education for an English child ...

14

If the educational time at our disposition were sufficient, there are one or two things I would add to those I have just now called the essentials; and perhaps you will be surprised to hear, though I hope you will not, that I should add, not more science, but one, or, if possible, two languages. The knowledge of some other language than one's own is, in fact, of singular intellectual value. Many of the faults and mistakes of the ancient philosophers are traceable to the fact that they knew no language but their own, and were often led into confusing the symbol with the thought which it embodied. I think it is Locke who says that one-half of the mistakes of philosophers have arisen from questions about words; and one of the safest ways of delivering yourself from the bondage of words is, to know how ideas look in words to which you are not accustomed. That is one reason for the study of language; another reason is, that it opens new fields in art and in science. Another is the practical value of such knowledge; and yet another is this, that if your languages are properly chosen, from the time of learning the additional languages you will know your own language better than ever you did ... Beyond these, the essential and the eminently desirable elements of all education, let each man take up his special line – the historian devote himself to his history, the man of science to his science, the man of letters to his culture of that kind, and the artist to his special pursuit.

Bacon has prefaced some of his works with no more than this: *Franciscus Bacon sic cogitavit;* let 'sic cogitavi' be the epilogue to what I have ventured to address to you to-night.

Collected Essays, III, 160–88
Address at prizegiving of the High School of the Liverpool Institution, 16 February 1883

ADDRESS ON BEHALF OF
THE NATIONAL ASSOCIATION
FOR THE PROMOTION
OF TECHNICAL EDUCATION
(1887)

It must be a matter of sincere satisfaction to those who, like myself, have for many years past been convinced of the vital importance of technical education to this country to see that that subject is now being taken up by some of the most important of our manufacturing towns. The... question has passed out of the region of speculation into that of action. I need hardly say to any one here that the task which our Association contemplates is not only one of primary importance – I may say of vital importance – to the welfare of the country; but that it is one of great extent and of vast difficulty. There is a well-worn adage that those who set out upon a great enterprise would do well to count the cost. I am not sure that this is always true. I think that some of the very greatest enterprises in this world have been carried out successfully simply because the people who undertook them did not count the cost; and I am much of opinion that, in this very case, the most instructive consideration for us is the cost of doing nothing. But there is one thing that is perfectly certain, and it is that, in undertaking all enterprises, one of the most important conditions of success is to have a perfectly clear comprehension of what you want to do...

Now, looking at the question of what we want to do in this broad and general way, it appears to me that it is necessary for us, in the first place, to amend and improve our system of primary education in such a fashion as will make it a proper preparation for the business of life. In the second place, I think we have to consider what measures may best be adopted for the development to its uttermost of that which may be called technical skill; and, in the third place, I think we have to consider what other matters there are for us to attend to, what other arrangements have to be kept carefully in sight in order that, while pursuing these ends, we do not forget that which is the end of civil existence, I mean a stable social state without which all other measures are merely futile, and, in effect, modes of going faster to ruin.

You are aware – no people should know the fact better than Manchester people – that, within the last seventeen years, a vast system of primary education has been created and extended over the whole country. I had some part in the original organisation of this system in London, and I am glad to think that, after all these years, I can look back upon that period of my life as perhaps the part of it least wasted.

No one can doubt that this system of primary education has done wonders for our population; but, from our point of view, I do not think anybody can doubt that it still has very considerable defects. It has the defect which is common to all the educational systems which we have inherited – it is too bookish, too little practical. The child is brought too little into contact with actual facts and things ... You know it was said of Dean Swift that he could write an admirable poem upon a broomstick, and the man who has a real knowledge of science can make the commonest object in the world subservient to an introduction to the principles and greater truths of natural knowledge. It is in that way that your science must be taught if it is to be of real service. Do not suppose any amount of book work, any repetition by rote of catechisms and other abominations of that kind are of value for our object. That is mere wasting of time ...

Now let me pass to my second point, which is the development of technical skill. Everybody here is aware that at this present moment there is hardly a branch of trade or of commerce which does not depend, more or less directly, upon some department or other of physical science, which does not involve, for its successful pursuit, reasoning from scientific data. Our machinery, our chemical processes or dyeworks, and a thousand operations which it is not necessary to mention, are all directly and immediately connected with science. You have to look among your workmen and foremen for persons who shall intelligently grasp the modifications, based upon science, which are constantly being introduced into these industrial processes. I do not mean that you want professional chemists, or physicists, or mathematicians, or the like, but you want people sufficiently familiar with the broad principles which underlie industrial operations to be able to adapt themselves to new conditions. Such qualifications can only be secured by a sort of scientific instruction which occupies a midway place between those primary notions given in the elementary schools and those more advanced studies which would be carried out in the technical schools...

Supposing we have this teaching of what I may call intermediate science, what we want next is technical instruction, in the strict sense of the word technical; I mean instruction in that kind of knowledge which is essential to the successful prosecution of the several branches of trade and industry. Now, the best way of obtaining this end is a matter about which the most experienced persons entertain very diverse opinions...

I suppose the best of all possible organisations is that of a school attached to a factory, where the employer has an interest in seeing that the instruction given is of a thoroughly practical kind, and where the pupils pass gradually by successive stages to the position of actual workmen...

I don't believe that the man lives at this present time who is competent to organise a final system of technical education. I believe that all attempts made in that direction must for many years to come be experimental, and that we must get to success through a series of blunders. Now that work is far better performed by private enterprise than in any other way. But there is another method which I think is permissible, and not only permissible but highly recommendable in this case, and that is the method of allowing the locality itself in which any branch of industry is pursued to be its own judge of its own wants, and to tax itself under certain conditions for the purpose of carrying out any scheme of technical education adapted to its needs. I am aware that there are many extreme theorists of the individualist school who hold that all this is very wicked and very wrong, and that by leaving things to themselves they will get right. Well, my experience of the world is that things left to themselves don't get right. I believe it to be sound doctrine that a municipality – and the State itself for that matter – is a corporation existing for the benefit of its members, and that here, as in all other cases, it is for the majority to determine that which is for the good of the whole, and to act upon that . . .

Another very important point in this connection is the question of the supply of teachers. I should say that is one of the greatest difficulties which beset the whole problem before us. I do not wish in the slightest degree to criticise the existing system of preparing teachers for ordinary school work. I have nothing to say about it. But what I do wish to say, and what I trust I may impress upon your minds firmly is this, that for the purpose of obtaining persons competent to teach science or to act as technical teachers, a different system must be adopted. For this purpose . . . the system of catching a boy or girl young, making a pupil teacher of him, compelling the poor little mortal to pour from his little bucket, into a still smaller bucket, that which has just been poured into it out of a big bucket; and passing him afterwards through the training college, where his life is devoted to filling the bucket from the pump from morning till night, without time for thought or reflection, is a system which should not continue ... For science teachers must have knowledge, and knowledge is not to be acquired on these terms. The power of repetition is, but that is not knowledge...

And there is another difficulty, namely, that when you have got your science or technical teacher it may not be easy to keep him. You have educated a man – a clever fellow very likely – on the understanding that he is to be a teacher. But the business of teaching is not a very lucrative and not a very attractive one, and an able man who has had a good training is under extreme temptations to carry his knowledge and his skill to a better market, in which case you have had all your trouble for nothing. It has often occurred to me that probably nothing would be of more service in this matter than the creation of a number of not very large bursaries ... to be held for a certain term of years, during which the holders should be bound to teach. I believe that some measure of this kind would do more to secure a good supply of teachers than anything else...

There remains yet one other matter which I think is of profound importance, perhaps of more importance than all the rest ... It is the need, while doing all these things, of keeping an eye, and an anxious eye, upon those measures which are necessary for the preservation of that stable and sound condition of the whole social organism which is the essential condition of real progress, and a chief end of all education. You will all recollect that some time ago there was a scandal and a great outcry about certain cutlasses and bayonets which had been supplied to our troops and sailors. These warlike implements were polished as bright as rubbing could make them; they were very well sharpened; they looked lovely. But when they were applied to the test of the work of war they broke and they bent, and proved more likely to hurt the hand of him that used them than to do any harm to the enemy. Let me apply that analogy to the effect of education, which is a sharpening and polishing of the mind. You may develop the intellectual side of people as far as you like, and you may confer upon them all the skill that training and instruction can give; but, if there is not, underneath all that outside form and superficial polish, the firm fibre of healthy manhood and earnest desire to do well, your labour is absolutely in vain...

Our sole chance of succeeding in a competition, which must constantly become more and more severe, is that our people shall not only have the knowledge and the skill which are required, but that they shall have the will and the energy and the honesty, without which neither knowledge nor skill can be of any permanent avail. This is what I mean by a stable social condition, because any other condition than this, any social condition in which the development of wealth involves the misery, the physical weakness, and the degradation of the worker, is absolutely and infallibly doomed to collapse. Your bayonets and cutlasses will break under your hand, and there will go on accumulating in society a mass of hopeless, physically incompetent, and morally degraded people, who are, as it were, a sort of dynamite which, sooner or later, when its accumulation becomes sufficient and its tension intolerable, will burst the whole fabric...

Collected Essays, III, 427–51
Address at inaugural meeting of National Association for the Advancement of Technical Education, Manchester Town Hall, 29 November 1887
Summary in *The Times* (30 November 1887)

THE STRUGGLE FOR EXISTENCE
IN HUMAN SOCIETY

(1888)

There are now 36,000,000 of people in our islands, and
every year considerably more than 300,000 are added to our
numbers. That is to say, about every hundred seconds, or
so, a new claimant to a share in the common stock of
maintenance presents him or herself among us. At the
present time, the produce of the soil does not suffice to feed
half its population. The other moiety has to be supplied
with food which must be bought from the people of food-
producing countries. That is to say, we have to offer
them the things which they want in exchange for the things
we want. And the things they want and which we can
produce better than they can are mainly manufactures –
industrial products.

The insolent reproach of the first Napoleon had a very
solid foundation. We not only are, but, under penalty of
starvation, we are bound to be, a nation of shopkeepers.
But other nations also lie under the same necessity of
keeping shop, and some of them deal in the same goods as
ourselves...

Let us be under no illusions, then. So long as unlimited
multiplication goes on, no social organisation which has
ever been devised, or is likely to be devised, no fiddle-
faddling with the distribution of wealth, will deliver society
from the tendency to be destroyed by the reproduction
within itself, in its intensest form, of that struggle for
existence the limitation of which is the object of society...
It is the true riddle of the Sphinx; and every nation which

does not solve it will sooner or later be devoured by the monster itself has generated . . .

Any one who is acquainted with the state of the population of all great industrial centres, whether in this or other countries, is aware that, amidst a large and increasing body of that population, *la misère* reigns supreme . . . Argumentation can hardly be needful to make it clear that no society in which the elements of decomposition are thus swiftly and surely accumulating can hope to win in the race of industries.

Intelligence, knowledge, and skill are undoubtedly conditions of success; but of what avail are they likely to be unless they are backed up by honesty, energy, goodwill, and all the physical and moral faculties that go to the making of manhood, and unless they are stimulated by hope of such reward as men may fairly look to ? . . .

Assuming that the physical and moral well-being and the stable social order, which are the indispensable conditions of permanent industrial development, are secured, there remains for consideration the means of attaining that knowledge and skill without which, even then, the battle of competition cannot be successfully fought. Let us consider how we stand. A vast system of elementary education has now been in operation among us for sixteen years, and . . . on the whole, it has worked well . . . But, as might be expected, it exhibits the defects of all our educational systems – . . . it has too much to do with books and too little to do with things . . . And it is not so much in the interests of industry, as in that of breadth of culture that I echo the common complaint against the bookish and theoretical character of our primary instruction . . .

There really is no reason why drawing should not be universally taught, and it is an admirable training for both eye and hand . . . In the next place, no good reason, except the want of capable teachers, can be assigned why elementary notions of science should not be an element in general instruction . . . The commonest thing – a candle, a boy's squirt, a piece of chalk – in the hands of a teacher who knows his business, may be made the starting-points whence children may be led into the regions of science . . . If object lessons often prove trivial failures, it is not the fault of the object lessons, but that of the teacher, who has not found out how much the power of teaching a little depends on knowing a great deal, and that thoroughly . . .

Technical education, in the strict sense, has become a necessity for two reasons. The old apprenticeship system has broken down, [and] . . . Invention is constantly changing the face of our industries, so that 'use and wont', 'rule of thumb', and the like, are gradually losing their importance, while that knowledge of principles which alone can deal successfully with changed conditions is becoming more and more valuable . . . The instruction formerly given by the master must therefore be more than replaced by the systematic teaching of the technical school . . .

We are here, as in all other questions of social organization, met by two diametrically opposed views. On the one hand, the methods pursued in foreign countries are held up as our example. The State is exhorted to take the matter in hand, and establish a great system of technical education. On the other hand, many economists of the individualist school exhaust the resources of language in condemning and repudiating, not merely the interference of the general [central] government in such matters, but the application of a farthing of the funds raised by local taxation to these purposes. I entertain a strong conviction that, in this country, at any rate, the State [centrally] had much better leave purely technical and trade instruction alone.

But . . . my individualism is rather of a sentimental sort, and I sometimes think I should be stronger in the faith if it were less vehemently advocated . . .

I cannot speak of my own knowledge, but I have every reason to believe that I came into this world a small reddish person, certainly without a gold spoon in my mouth, and in fact with no discernible abstract or concrete 'rights' or property of any description . . . If I was nourished, cared for, taught, saved from the vagabondage of a wastrel, I certainly am not aware that I did anything to deserve these advantages . . . So that if society, having, quite gratuitously, done all these things for me, asks me in turn to do something towards its preservation – even if that something is to contribute to the teaching of other men's children – I really, in spite of all my individualist leanings, feel rather ashamed to say no . . .

It does not appear to me, then, that there is any valid objection to taxation for purposes of education; but, in the case of technical schools and classes, I think it is practically expedient that such a taxation should be local. Our industrial population accumulates in particular towns and districts; these districts are those which immediately profit by technical education; and it is only in them that we can find the men practically engaged in industries, among whom some may reasonably be expected to be competent judges of that which is wanted, and of the best means of meeting the want.

In my belief, all methods of technical training are at present tentative, and, to be successful, each must be adapted to the special peculiarities of its locality. This is a case in which we want twenty years, not of 'strong government', but of cheerful and hopeful blundering; and we may be thankful if we get things straight in that time . . .

Supposing our intermediate science teaching and our technical schools and classes are established, there is yet a third need to be supplied, and that is the want of good teachers. And it is necessary not only to get them, but to keep them when you have got them.

It is impossible to insist too strongly upon the fact that efficient teachers of science and of technology are not to be made by the processes in vogue at ordinary training colleges. The memory loaded with mere bookwork is not the thing wanted – is, in fact, rather worse than useless – in the teacher of scientific subjects. It is absolutely essential that his mind should be full of knowledge and not of mere learning, and that what he knows should have been learned in the laboratory rather than in the library ... But when the well-trained men are supplied, it must be recollected that the profession of teacher is not a very lucrative or otherwise tempting one, and that it may be advisable to offer special inducements to good men to remain in it...

Last, but not least, comes the question of providing the machinery for enabling those who are by nature specially qualified to undertake the higher branches of industrial work, to reach the position in which they may render that service to the community. If all our educational expenditure did nothing but pick one man of scientific or inventive genius, each year, from amidst the hewers of wood and drawers of water, and give him the chance of making the best of his inborn faculties, it would be a very good investment. If there is one such child among the hundreds of thousands of our annual increase, it would be worth any money to drag him either from the slough of misery, or from the hotbed of wealth, and teach him to devote himself to the service of his people...

The thing can be done; I have endeavoured to show good grounds for the belief that it must be done, and that speedily, if we wish to hold our own in the war of industry. I doubt not that it will be done, whenever its absolute necessity becomes as apparent to all those who are absorbed in the actual business of industrial life as it is to some of the lookers on...

Collected Essays, IX, 195–236

Published in *The Nineteenth Century*, XXIII (February 1888), 161 under the title, 'The Struggle for Existence: a Programme'

Reprinted with additional note in T. H. Huxley, *Social Diseases and Worse Remedies* (Macmillan, 1891)

CHRONOLOGY

1825   Thomas Henry Huxley born at Ealing, Middlesex, of George and Rachel (née Withers) Huxley, 4 May.

1826   'London University' (University College) founded; Society for Diffusion of Useful Knowledge founded.

1827   Thomas Arnold appointed to Rugby.

1828   University College School founded.

1829   King's College, London, founded (opened 1831).

1830   Public schools and universities under heavy criticism.

1831   British Association for Advancement of Science founded; Board of Education for Ireland established.

1832   University of Durham founded (chartered 1837); rebellion at Eton; *Penny Magazine* started; first Reform Act trebled electorate to ¾ million.

1833   T.H.H. entered Ealing School.
£20,000 Parliamentary grant for schools; *Penny Cyclopaedia* started.

1835   T.H.H. left school (family moved to Coventry).
Government School of Design established; Municipal Reform Act (Borough Councils established).

1836   Examining University of London founded.

1837   T.H.H. reading Hutton's *Geology*, Hamilton's *Logic*, Carlyle's *French Revolution;* learning German.

1839   T.H.H.'s sisters, Eliza and Ellen, married.

1840   T.H.H. began *Thoughts and Doings* (→1845); reading science and philosophy; learning French and Latin.
Battersea Training College (St John's) founded.

1841   T.H.H. began medical apprenticeship in Rotherhithe; reading for matriculation.
St Mark's Training College (Chelsea) founded; over 200 Mechanics' Institutes functioning.

1842   T.H.H. gained free scholarship to Charing Cross Hospital (→1845); awarded silver medal (Apothecaries' Hall) for Botany.
Chartist riots; income tax 7*d*. in £.

1843   T.H.H. awarded prizes (Charing Cross) in Chemistry, Anatomy and Physiology; reading Carlyle's *Past and Present*.
Ethnological Society founded.

1845   T.H.H. gained first M.B. (London University) with gold medal for Anatomy and Physiology; first research paper published.

       22 teacher-training colleges functioning in England and Wales.

1846   T.H.H. entered Royal Naval Medical Service as assistant-surgeon; sailed on *Rattlesnake*, 3 December.

       College of Preceptors founded; pupil-teacher system established.

1847   T.H.H. met Henrietta Anne Heathorn (future wife) in Sydney; working on medusae, etc.

1848   T.H.H. packeting research papers to England in hope of publication.

       Queen's College (for women), London, founded; end of Chartism; *Communist Manifesto* (Marx and Engels) published.

1849   T.H.H. continuing researches; learning Italian.

       Over 700 Mechanics' Institutes functioning.

1850   T.H.H. returned to England, 23 October; granted special leave for research (→1853).

       Government School of Mines (Jermyn Street) founded; Royal Commissions on Oxford and Cambridge appointed; Natural Science Honours School established at Oxford.

1851   T.H.H. elected Fellow of Royal Society.

       Owens College (future university) founded at Manchester; Cheltenham Ladies College founded; Natural Sciences Tripos established at Cambridge; Great Exhibition at Crystal Palace.

1852   T.H.H.'s mother died; awarded gold medal of Royal Society.

       Science and Art Department established under Board of Trade.

1853   T.H.H.'s research leave terminated.

       Maurice's Working Men's College founded; £260,000 Parliamentary grant for schools.

1854   T.H.H. struck off Navy List; appointed to School of Mines at £200 per annum; working mainly on fossils; lecturing for Department of Science and Art, etc.; 'Educational Value of Natural History Sciences'.

       Newman Rector of Dublin (Roman Catholic) University.

1855　T.H.H.'s father died; married Miss Heathorn; salary raised to £600 per annum; Fullerian Professor at Royal Institution (→1858 and 1865-8).

　　　Society of Arts examinations started.

1856　T.H.H.'s son, Noel, born; lectures to London working men; examiner to University of London (→1870); Fellow of Zoological Society and Geological Society; 'Natural History as Knowledge, Discipline and Power.'

　　　£451,000 Parliamentary grant for schools; Life Peerages suggested.

1857　T.H.H. beginning tendency to hypochondria; honorary fellowships of various British and foreign scientific societies (accumulating rapidly during next ten years and then at intervals throughout life).

　　　Indian Mutiny (→1858).

1858　T.H.H.'s daughter, Jessie, born; Croonian Lecturer; elected to Athenaeum; Fellow of Linnean Society.

　　　Oxford and Cambridge Local Examinations established.

1859　T.H.H.'s daughter, Marian, born; Secretary of Geological Society (→1862).

　　　Newcastle Commission on Elementary Education (→1861); Science and Art Department grants for science teaching started; Robert Lowe Vice-President of Committee of Council on Education; Darwin's *Origin of Species* published; Fears of war in Europe.

1860　T.H.H.'s son, Noel, died; Leonard born; British Association 'duel' with Bishop of Oxford.

　　　Science degrees established at University of London.

1861　T.H.H. conducted Teachers' Course at South Kensington; honorary Ph.D. of Breslau; 'Lobster...Study of Zoology'.

　　　Clarendon Commission on Public Schools (→1864); Lowe's Revised Code; Matthew Arnold's *Popular Education of France* and Herbert Spencer's *Education* published; American Civil War (→1865).

1862　T.H.H.'s daughter, Rachel, born; Hunterian Professor at Royal College of Surgeons (→1869); member of Royal Commission on Scottish Herring Trawling Acts.

　　　Hartley Institution (future university) opened at Southampton; 'Payment by Results' introduced; Kay-Shuttleworth's *Four Periods of Public Education* published.

1863　T.H.H.'s daughter, Nettie, born; working especially on

15

human fossils; lectures to general public at School of Mines; *Man's Place in Nature*.

'New Code' introduced.

1864   T.H.H. member of Royal Commission on Sea Fisheries (→1865); *X* Club formed.

Bedford College (for women) established in London; Taunton Commission on Endowed Schools (→1867); Argyll Commission on Scottish Schools (→1867); Robert Lowe resigned; Co-operative Wholesale Society founded.

1865   T.H.H.'s son, Henry, born; Governor of International College, Isleworth; 'Emancipation – Black and White'.

St Pancras station built.

1866   T.H.H.'s daughter, Ethel, born; member of Commission on Royal College of Science for Ireland; President of Section D of British Association; honorary LL.D. of Edinburgh; member of 'Jamaica Committee' to prosecute Governor Eyre for murder; *Elementary Physiology* and 'Advisableness of Improving Natural Knowledge'.

International College (Isleworth) opened.

1867   T.H.H. working especially on anthropology and ethnology (→1871) and on classification of birds.

Essays on a Liberal Education published; second Reform Act; Canadian Federation formed.

1868   T.H.H. first Principal of South London Working Men's College (→1880); President of Ethnological Society (→1871); member of Commission on Science and Art Education in Ireland; 'A Liberal Education . . .'

Public Schools Act; Select Committee on Scientific Instruction; Mark Pattison's *Academical Organisation* and Matthew Arnold's *Schools on the Continent* published; end of public executions; Disraeli Prime Minister.

1869   T.H.H. coined word 'agnostic'; President of Geological Society (→1871); member of Metaphysical Society; science lessons to London schoolchildren; 'Scientific Education'.

Girton College founded at Hitchin; Headmasters' Conference founded; Endowed Schools Act; Matthew Arnold's *Culture and Anarchy* and J. S. Mill's *Subjection of Women* published; Trades Union Congress founded; Gladstone Prime Minister.

1870 T.H.H. elected to first London School Board; President of British Association; Governor of Owens College (→1875); member of Royal Commission on Contagious Diseases Acts (→1871) and Royal ('Devonshire') Commission on Scientific Instruction (→1875); lecturing widely about country to literary and philosophical societies, working men's clubs, etc.; 'The School Boards...' and 'On Medical Education'.

School of Mines began move to South Kensington; Forster's Education Act; National Union of Teachers founded; Franco-Prussian War; Vatican Council.

1871 T.H.H. elected Secretary of Royal Society (→1880); refused to stand for Parliament; conducted first practical course for teachers at South Kensington; 'Administrative Nihilism'.

Newnham College founded; University Tests Act (removing some religious tests); International Education Exhibition; Bank Holidays Act; Germany unified.

1872 T.H.H. seriously ill; convalescence in Egypt and Italy; elected Rector of Aberdeen University (→1875).

Chair of Education established at College of Preceptors; Girls' Public Day School Company (later, Trust) founded; Samuel Butler's *Erewhon* published; secret ballot introduced.

1873 Cambridge University Extension lectures started.

1874 T.H.H.'s health much better; 'Universities: Actual and Ideal' and 'Hypothesis that Animals are Automata...'

Yorkshire College (future university) founded at Leeds; Disraeli Prime Minister.

1875 T.H.H. appointed Professor *locum tenens* at Edinburgh (and 1876); *Practical Elementary Biology*.

London Medical School for Women founded.

1876 T.H.H. gave opening address at Johns Hopkins University, Baltimore; Wollaston Medal; Vice-President of Working Men's Club and Institute Union; member of Royal Commission on Vivisection and Royal Commission on Universities of Scotland (→1878); 'Address on University Education' and 'On the Study of Biology'.

Peripatetic science teachers introduced in Liverpool schools; Bell invented telephone.

1877 T.H.H. advised City Companies on promotion of

technical education; *Physiography*. 'Elementary Instruction in Physiology' and 'Technical Education'.

Nineteenth Century started; Kay-Shuttleworth died.

1878 T.H.H.'s daughter, Jessie, married; Leonard to St Andrews; President of Queckett Microscopical Club (and 1879); honorary LL.D. of Dublin; learning Greek; working on crayfish and sensory physiology; *Hume*.

Maria Grey Training College (for women) founded; City and Guilds of London Institute founded; University of London degrees opened to women.

1879 T.H.H.'s daughter, Marian, married; Leonard to Oxford; Governor of Eton (→1888); honorary LL.D. of Cambridge; working on mammalian anatomy.

Firth College (future university) founded in Sheffield; Cambridge University Teachers' Training Syndicate appointed; popular interest shifting from religion to politics.

1880 T.H.H. awarded Clarke Medal; 'Science and Culture' and *Introductory Science Primer*.

Mason College (future university) founded in Birmingham; Owens College became Victoria University of Manchester; Salvation Army founded; Gladstone Prime Minister.

1881 T.H.H. became Dean of Normal School of Science (→1895); President of Sanitary Protection Association; Inspector of Salmon Fisheries (→1885); member of Royal Commission on Medical Acts (→1892); refused professor and head of house offers from Oxford.

School of Mines became Normal School of Science; University College (future university) founded in Liverpool; Commission ('Samuelson') on Technical Education (→1884); Cambridge Tripos examinations opened to women; Disraeli died.

1882 T.H.H. rejected $10,000 per annum to go to Harvard; honorary M.D. of Würtzburg; working especially on fish diseases.

Regent Street Polytechnic opened; British control of Egypt; Darwin died.

1883 T.H.H. elected President of Royal Society (→1886); Fellow of Royal College of Surgeons; Trustee of British Museum (→1886 and 1888-95); Senator of London University (→1895); Rede Lecturer at Cambridge;

'Science and Art in Relation to Education'.

Finsbury Technical College opened in City; London University Diploma in Education established; Maxim invented automatic gun; Karl Marx died.

1884 T.H.H.'s ill-health became chronic; daughter, Rachel, married; Vice-President of Society of Authors; member of Royal Commission on Trawl Fishing; resigned Presidency of National Association of Science Teachers.

City and Guilds College opened in South Kensington; *Oxford English Dictionary* and *Agnostic Annual* started; third Reform Act; Fabian Society and Social Democratic Federation founded.

1885 T.H.H.'s son, Leonard, married; resigned Professorship at Normal School of Science; honorary D.C.L. of Oxford; began theological controversies with Gladstone.

Education grants totalled £3,000,000; *Dictionary of National Biography* started; Gordon relieved at Khartoum; Salisbury Prime Minister.

1886 T.H.H. to Switzerland for convalescence.

Gladstone Prime Minister.

1887 T.H.H.'s daughter, Marian, died; Julian Huxley born; gave up most examining; working on hybridism in gentians; 'Address on ... Technical Education'.

Royal Holloway College founded; People's Palace opened in East End; Commission ('Cross') on Technical Education (→1888); Queen Victoria's Golden Jubilee; Eiffel Tower erected; Salisbury Prime Minister.

1888 T.H.H.'s health very poor; Copley Medal; honorary M.D. of Bologna; President of International Geological Congress; 'Struggle for Existence in Human Society'.

Local Government Act established County Councils; Hertz produced radio waves; Matthew Arnold died.

1889 T.H.H.'s health improved slightly; daughters, Ethel and Nettie, married; moved to Eastbourne.

Universities (Scotland) Act; Technical Instruction Act.

1890 T.H.H. convalesced in Canaries; son, Harry, married; Linnean Medal; President of Palaeontographical Society (→1895).

Normal School of Science became Royal College of Science; University Day Training Departments founded in several cities; Newman died.

1891   T.H.H. still very poorly.
         Goldsmiths' College, London, opened.
1892   T.H.H. made Privy Councillor; busy with London
         University reform.
         Independent Labour Party formed; Gladstone Prime
         Minister.
1893   T.H.H. gave Romanes Lecture at Oxford; honorary
         M.D. of Erlangen; Hayden Medal.
         University of Wales founded; school-leaving age
         raised to eleven; Blind and Deaf Children Education
         Act.
1894   T.H.H. at British Association, Oxford; Darwin Medal;
         Aldous Huxley born.
         Commission ('Bryce') on Secondary Education (→ 1895);
         Rosebery Prime Minister.
1895   T.H.H. died at Eastbourne, 29 June; buried without
         religious ceremony at Finchley, 4 July.

GUIDE TO FURTHER READING

Huxley's work in and views on education were so much an integral part of his extraordinarily varied and vigorous life that they can only be seen in full context by those who have made some biographical study. The filial two-volume *Life and Letters of Thomas Henry Huxley*, by Leonard Huxley (Macmillan, 1909), is the basic source, but it has some errors and some strange omissions, and does less than justice to its subject's more radical attitudes and actions.

There have been a fair number of other biographies, but the only one to provide much fresh material and a major re-assessment is *T. H. Huxley: Scientist, Humanist and Educator*, by Cyril Bibby (London: Watts, and New York: Horizon Press, 1959). In addition, there is some interesting material, in the form of extracts from family letters and manuscript notes, in *The Essence of T. H. Huxley*, by Cyril Bibby (London: Macmillan, and New York: St Martin's Press, 1967). Those who have access to the University of London may also consult Bibby's 950-page typescript study, *T. H. Huxley: his Place in Education*, of which a copy was deposited in the Goldsmiths' Library in 1955.

Since Huxley never produced any major work synthesising his educational ideas, it is necessary for the research worker to probe into a great mass of material scattered among books, learned journals, quality periodicals, semi-popular magazines, the weekly and daily press, and unpublished manuscripts. However, a great deal can be garnered from the nine volumes of *Collected Essays*, by Thomas H. Huxley (Macmillan, 1893–4). These volumes are as follows:

I   *Method and Results*
II   *Darwiniana*
III   *Science and Education*
IV   *Science and Hebrew Tradition*
V   *Science and Christian Tradition*
VI   *Hume, with Helps to the Study of Berkeley*
VII   *Man's Place in Nature*
VIII   *Discourses, Biological and Geological*
IX   *Evolution and Ethics, and Other Essays*

It is also instructive to examine some of Huxley's less technical scientific books, such as:

Evidences as to Man's Place in Nature. Williams & Norgate, 1863.
Lessons in Elementary Physiology. Macmillan, 1866.
A Course of Practical Instruction in Elementary Biology. Macmillan 1875 (with H. N. Martin).
Physiography: an Introduction to the Study of Nature. Macmillan, 1877.
The Crayfish: an Introduction to the Study of Zoology. Kegan Paul, 1879.
Introductory Science Primer. Macmillan, 1880.

Even the non-scientist educator will find it worth while at least to glance at the above six volumes, so as to savour something of science education *à la Huxley.*

Particular aspects of Huxley's work in education are considered in the following papers by Cyril Bibby:

'The Huxley-Wilberforce Debate: a Postscript', *Nature*, CLXXVI, 20 August 1955, 363.
'T. H. Huxley and Education', *J. Educ.*, LXXXVII, December 1955, 535.
'The South London Working Men's College: a Forgotten Venture', *Adult Educ.*, XXVIII, Winter 1955, 211.
'T. H. Huxley and the Training of Teachers', *Educ. Rev.*, VIII, February 1956, 137.
'T. H. Huxley's Idea of a University', *Univ. Quart.*, X, August 1956, 377.
'The Imperial Institute: a Great Conception', *Vocational Aspect*, VIII, Autumn 1956, 111.
'T. H. Huxley and Technical Education', *J. R. Soc. Arts*, CIV, 14 September 1956, 810.
'T. H. Huxley and Medical Education', *Charing Cross Hosp. Gaz.*, LIV, October 1956, 191.
'A Victorian Experiment in International Education: the College at Spring Grove', *Brit. J. Educ. Studies*, V, November 1956, 25.
'Science as an Instrument of Culture: an Examination of the Views of T. H. Huxley', *Researches and Studies*, XV, January 1957, 7.
'The Prince of Controversialists', *Twentieth Cent.*, CLXI, March 1957, 268.

'T. H. Huxley and the Universities of Scotland', *Aberdeen Univ. Rev.*, XXXVII, Autumn 1957, 134.

'The First Year of the London School Board: the Dominant Role of T. H. Huxley', *Durham Research Rev.*, II, September 1957, 151.

'Thomas Henry Huxley and University Development', *Victorian Studies*, II, December 1958, 97.

'The Rôle of T. H. Huxley in the Development of Universities in the Nineteenth Century', *Educ. Rev.*, XI, February 1959, 139.

'T. H. Huxley and the University of Oxford', *Oxford Mag.*, 6 Hilary, 1 March 1968.

These papers provide between them such a range of references to original sources as to open virtually all paths to further study of T. H. Huxley as educator.

Finally, there is the rich mine of Huxley manuscripts and notebooks in the archives of the Imperial College of Science and Technology, to which warm acknowledgement is made for facilities granted.

INDEX